The Red Rugs of Tarsus

The Red Rugs of Tarsus

A Lady's Experiences in Turkey at the Time of the
Armenian Persecutions 1909-1914

Helen Davenport Gibbons

LEONAUR

The Red Rugs of Tarsus
A Lady's Experiences in Turkey at the Time of the Armenian Persecutions 1909-1914
by Helen Davenport Gibbons

First published under the title
The Red Rugs of Tarsus

Leonaur is an imprint of Oakpast Ltd

Copyright in this form © 2012 Oakpast Ltd

ISBN: 978-0-85706-984-9 (hardcover)
ISBN: 978-0-85706-985-6 (softcover)

http://www.leonaur.com

Publisher's Notes

Contents

To

The Memory of

C. H. M. Doughty-Wylie, V.C.

"The Major" of This Book

Who was killed in action leading a

charge on Gallipoli Peninsula,

April 29, 1915

Preface

When I was a freshman at Bryn Mawr I decided I should "write something." My girlhood was uneventful and joyous—the girlhood of the lucky American who has a wholesome good time. I knew I must wait for experience. I was too sensitive about my youth to expose what I was thinking, for fear "they" would know I was not grown up.

The experiences I was looking for came. They were so painful that seven years passed before I put pen to paper. Today, after the lapse of years, I am not sure that my perspective is good. In looking back upon those six weeks in Adana Province between April thirteenth and the end of May, nineteen-nine, they seem longer than all the rest of my life.

The thought of publishing I rejected and rejected again. I avoided dwelling on that time the way one puts off going back to a house one has not entered since a loved one died. To this day we have lived up to an agreement made back in those days, and my husband and I have never told each other the worst we know about the atrocities committed by the Turks.

But recent events in Armenia brought it all back again. My indignation, and a sense of duty and of pity, transcended all personal feelings. I lived again that night in Tarsus, when we—seven defenceless women, our one foreign man a brave young Swiss teacher of French, and 4,800 Armenians waited our turn at the hands of the Kurds.

Massacres had begun again, a thousand times worse than before. Other American women were in the same untold peril that I had been. The whole Armenian people were marked for extermination. Now, as then, help had to come. But from where? What could I do? I could not go out there. I had my four babies. I had four hundred and fifty French soldiers' babies I had been mothering since the war began.

I had no time to write a book, although the old Freshman ambition still existed. I had been waiting ever since my marriage in nineteen-eight for a quiet time to come when I could settle down and cultivate a literary instinct, but the chance never came. Our honeymoon had never finished—it hasn't yet. I had set up six homes in seven years. We had lived in Tarsus (Armenia), Paris, Constantinople, Paris again, Princeton (New Jersey), and then settled in Paris for the third time.

In Tarsus we went through the massacres of April, 1909, when thirty thousand Armenians were slaughtered by the Turks in Adana Province alone. My first baby was born on May 5th that year, under martial law, in a little Armenian town that was only saved from similar experiences by the protecting guns of the warships of seven nations. At the end of that year we had settled in our first apartment in Paris, and Christmas was no sooner past than we had the famous flood of 1910, when a quarter of the city was under water.

There was nothing dull about our life of three years in Constantinople. First came the cholera epidemic; the *effendi*, my little son, was born in a house where the neighbours on one side had cholera and those on the other side smallpox. Then the war between Turkey and Italy; more cholera; huge fires which destroyed whole quarters of the city; and finally the First Balkan War, when ten thousand wounded men came into the city in a single day, St. Sophia was filled with a mixture of thousands of refugees and cholera stricken soldiers, and I sheltered myself from a west wind on a hillside above my home and listened with grim satisfaction to the Christian guns of the Balkan Allies thundering at the gates of the city.

Then the *chellabi* [1] sent me back to Paris, to find an apartment near the Bibliothèque National. Kitty Giggles and the *effendi* had ordered a new sister, who was to be called Mignonne, and if she was not to be born in Constantinople the sooner I got to Paris the better. Mignonne and I were scarcely home from the Paris hospital than the Second Balkan War broke out—and the *chellabi* was down in Albania. He had to decide whether he would stay there and follow the Serbian Army in the field, or come back through the thick of it to me and the baby daughter he had never seen and the musty old manuscripts in the Bibliothèque. It took him a month to get through, while I waited in Paris without news of him.

October that year found us in Princeton, New Jersey. Friends at

1. *Chellabi*—Turkish for "master of the house."

home pleaded that we had been away five years, and it was time we came back to them. At Princeton, which has the second purest water supply in the world, Kitty Giggles and the *effendi* in some mysterious way were struck down with typhoid, and four months of anxiety taught us that war is nothing compared to a sick baby. By a miracle both recovered, and May, 1914, found us all happily playing on the beach in Brittany.

In a few weeks our first real vacation was suddenly brought to an end by the beginning of the great European War, and the *chellabi* had to leave hastily for Paris, alone, on Mobilisation Day. All the babies in the little Breton village, including my own three, were down with whooping-cough. The following seven weeks down there were a circus. I did everything, from mending the skull of a peasant woman who fell downstairs in a fit of drunken grief to acting as unofficial *maire* of the commune and making out *permis de séjour* and passports for the *maire's adjoint* to stamp.

The journey back to Paris in the same month as the Battle of the Marne was comparatively easy, as most of the traffic was in the opposite direction. The two years since then, in this heroine city of Paris in wartime have been an unforgettable experience, in which both fatigue and leisure have alike been impossible. The "Ickle One" came into the world last November, to find her mother deep in baby relief work. Her real name is "Hope," because of my belief that the great hope of France and of the world is in the new generation.

Now it is eight years that we have been inhabiting storm centres, and I have come to believe that my function is to create a normal home atmosphere in abnormal conditions.

The book I have dreamed of has never been written. The appeal on my sympathies made by the sufferings of the Armenians of today, (as at time of first publication), however, required that something should be done. For this reason I have resurrected the old and yellowed letters which I wrote to my mother during that agonizing time in Tarsus. Portions of them have been rewritten, and certain intimate details in which the public can have no interest have been cut out, and I have occasionally added a few explanatory details to make things clearer to the general reader. I now send them out in the hope that the plain story of one American woman's experiences will bring home to other American women and to American men the reality and the awfulness of these massacres and the heroism of the American missionaries, who, in many cases, have lain down their lives in defence of their Armenian friends and fellow Christians.

Technically speaking, we were not missionaries. We went to Tarsus at the invitation of Dr. Thomas Davidson Christie, the President of the college there, to spend a year rendering what service we could to the regularly appointed missionaries; therefore I am at liberty to express, as I did above, my admiration for the American missionaries from a purely impartial standpoint.

CHAPTER 1

Half Way Through the First Year

Tarsus, Turkey-in-Asia,
December second,
Nineteen-Eight.

Mother dear:

My first married birthday! I am twenty-six years old. It is twenty-six weeks since The Day. I have been counting up the different places at which we stopped on the way from New York to Tarsus. This is the twenty-sixth abode we have occupied in the twenty-six weeks. Isn't that a coincidence? You are smiling and saying that it is just like honeymooners to notice it at all.

Wish you could sit beside me near our big log fire in the bedroom. The fireplace is made of solid stone, and in it we burn whole logs. When the wind is blowing a certain direction, puffs come down the chimney and the smoke nearly chokes me. It is good for us that this is only an occasional happening. Herbert insists solemnly that the smoke of a wood fire is good for the eyes. Even with his eyes smarting and half-shut, I can see him twinkle and know that he is teasing.

I am training myself to look after every little detail in the care of our rooms. In the morning I put all "in good order." Chips are picked up and thrown into the woodbox. Tumblers and mirror polished, every corner dusted. 'No meals for me to think about: for the mission family eats in the college dining-room.

Each of the three young couples in this house has what Mother Christie calls a houseboy. That means a student who is making his own way. Ours is a Greek about sixteen years old, whose tuition we pay. He gives us two hours' work each day. Socrates makes our fires, puts the saddles on our horses, brings water, and goes to the market to fetch oranges (of which I eat an inordinate number). A fire is made

13

under a huge kettle, like my grandmother's apple-butter boiler, and hot water is obtained in this way for our baths. If we want a bath at night, Socrates starts the fire at supper-time, and brings us the water during the little recess he has between two evening study hours. He keeps my bottle of alcohol filled with the pure grape spirits people make here. I get an *oke* at a time (a quart is about four cups, isn't it? Well, an *oke* is about five). I have a basket for big Jaffa oranges and another for mandarines.

Socrates interprets well when we go shopping. He is certainly a handy boy. We help him with his lessons sometimes. When he cleaned our room the first Saturday, he asked me "to arrange all those funny pretty things," pointing to silver toilet articles, "just the way you want them kept." When it was done, he spent a long time walking slowly around the place. He memorized my arrangement, and has not slipped up a single Saturday since. When we take a horseback ride Saturday morning, part of the fun of that ride is the thought that when we get back to our rooms, they will have been beautifully cleaned and everything will look just right for Sunday.

On the outside wall of our bedroom, directly behind the head of our bed, and covering the entire space between two windows, is a very large red and blue *kileem*. On the floor are square blue rugs, just the shade to make Herbert imagine my eyes are not green. On one side Mrs. Christie has had two cedar wardrobes built in, and between them are a whole lot of drawers, up to dressing-table height. Back of the door, leading from the bedroom to the study, is a table where I have the First Aid outfit Dr. Oliver Smith gave me for my wedding gift.

Socrates confided in me that he wants to be a doctor. He comes from a Greek village in the heart of the silver mine district of the Taurus. His father and mother died during an epidemic. He tells me that he knew, young as he was, that if there had been a doctor in his village, his parents might not have died; and that he had determined then to be a doctor, so that other little boys might not lose their parents.

Doctor Christie told the boys in chapel one morning that when they got hurt they could come to me for bandaging. Herbert teases me about the miles and miles of bandages in my professional-looking japanned tin box. There is a wonderful case of medicine. Those I do not know how to use I have put away up high on a shelf in case I might sometime lend them to the doctor. The things I know how to use are kept in first-class order by Socrates. I bought a little white

14

enamelled basin or two to be used when I make dressings. For six weeks I have been taking care of an ugly open sore on the leg of one of my students. It is a case of cotton poisoning. These people get cotton poisoning by contact with the plant at picking-time. I never heard of it before, but I used my head, cleaned the sore with camphenol, and have dressed it with camphenol-soaked bandages twice every day. I was rewarded after a week in seeing the wound surrounded by a ring of nice clean flesh. The infected part has been diminishing in size, and within the past few days is completely covered with a layer of new skin. I am proud of this: for the boy could not walk very well when he first came to me.

Last Sunday Melanchthon, a kid of fourteen, nearly amputated his finger in the bread-cutter. I fixed it up with adhesive tape stitches placed all around the cut, until the doctor could get back from some distant village to sew it. Thank Heaven, Melanchthon can still wiggle his finger joint. When Socrates took him back to the dormitory after I had dressed his finger that first day, the little fellow asked if he could go to see the lady again. Socrates explained that the lady had said he must return on the morrow for another dressing. Melanchthon was pleased. He did want to see the pretty room again. He wondered if Sultan Abdul Hamid had anything so fine in Yildiz Kiosk.

Eflaton (Armenian for Plato), a nearsighted chap in my sub-freshman class, was working with a bunch of boys at the corner of the yard, where a wee bit of wall is being built. Some day there may be money to put the wall all around the college property. It grows almost imperceptibly as gifts for that purpose come in. They are few, alas! Just a tiny corner is finished. The boys were piling stone, and Eflaton had the ill-luck to get two fingers of his right hand badly crushed. Again the doctor was far away, and I did my best. Today, when I had finished Eflaton's dressing, he looked up at me with those dreamy eyes of his and announced, "Mrs. Gibbons, you are a angel!" When I protested that I was not "a angel," he agreed with me. Because, said he, "You are better than that: you are a angel mother." Oh, these honey-tongued Orientals! They beat the Irish.

The trip planned by Henri Imer and Herbert to Namroun has not yet come off. They intended to leave towards the end of the last week of October, returning the following Tuesday. Wives were to take their classes. Before the bad weather set in, we were anxious to have Henri take for us a lot of photographs of the acropolis and castle there. All plans were made to go. But political news prevented their leaving. The action of Bulgaria and Austria has raised a ferment throughout Turkey, especially in these parts, where there are many Armenian Christians. A reactionary movement is feared. The Armenians fear that the Mohammedans distrust their loyalty.

The fasting month of *Ramazan* ended on October twenty-fifth, and the following Monday the great *Bairam* (feast) began. Lower-class Mohammedans generally get gloriously drunk in towns on this day. Occidental Turkophiles write of and praise Moslems as being the original White Ribboners. Perhaps many are, but not town Turks, who consume quantities of *raki*, the strongest fire-water man ever invented. During this *Bairam* the Armenians were fearing a massacre. The constitution has lifted the prohibition of owning firearms. We hear the Armenians have been buying in large quantities. We did not ourselves anticipate trouble. But one never knows in this country. It was best for Henri and Herbert not to go.

I am soon for bed. We must be up by six. At least I suppose it is six. The way they tell time here makes me dizzy. So many hours since sunrise, they say. Or, so many hours since sunset. The precise minute for doing any given thing must be worked out the way they make a time-table at the sea-shore, to show you when to take your swim. The mischief of it is, of course, that the time-table varies each day. The night we arrived in Tarsus, after our weeks of camping in the Taurus, we rode our tired horses under the arch of the college gate at ten p.m. The silly clock in a tower nearby was striking four.

I am not sure whether the East or the West knows the philosophical way to tell time. Perhaps Western reckoning tends to be too precise, and Greenwich time is contrary to nature. Anyhow, the Eastern way would make an efficiency expert's work-schedule look like a cinema film run by a greenhorn. Perhaps these Eastern peoples who dream dreams and feed their souls on starlight must map out their day by the going of the sun.

CHAPTER 2

Three Christmases and the Seven Sleepers

Tarsus,
December twenty-fifth.

Dearest Mother:

College classes going at full swing today. It is not Christmas for the boys. Some of the early missionaries to Turkey had it in their noddle that December twenty-fifth was really the day Christ was born, and they were shocked to see the Greeks celebrating January sixth and the Armenians January nineteenth. Missionaries were unimaginative, too, wrapped up in their own narrow ideas, too sure they were right and all the rest of mankind wrong (else why had they sacrificed everything to come way out here?) to realize that the Eastern calendar is thirteen days behind ours.

The missionaries couldn't call the Greek aberration a sin. They could not logically hold out for a calendar made in Rome! But they did get after their Armenian converts on the theological question, and for many years insisted on an American celebration. Absurdities like that have now happily passed in missionary work, and your missionary of today is better able to distinguish between essentials and non-essentials than the old-fashioned Puritans, who were every bit as bigoted as medieval Catholics.

But I am getting away from Christmas in Asia! Herbert and I taught our classes this morning as usual. We are going to celebrate tonight. We have a turkey roasting, and there is a jar of cranberry sauce that did not arrive in time for Thanksgiving. I have just come from the kitchen, flushed with the stove and the triumph of having really succeeded in doing the trick I learned at Simmons College last year.

17

My fruits and nuts are genuinely *glacéd*,

If I haven't lived up to Simmons College cookery, Mother, I've made some use of Bryn Mawr. Herbert's schedule is twenty-five hours a week. What time was there left for private study? To take advantage of next year in Paris, he simply must do some ground-work on his fellowship thesis. So I have taken over ten of his hours—the two English courses: preparatory boys learning the first rudiments of our language, and—joy of joys!—his sub-freshman class. They know pretty well how to speak and write English, so I am giving them rhetoric—and incidentally I am getting myself more than I give. One has to teach to learn!

I have kidnapped that sub-freshman class, and Herbert will not get them back. I may grow weary of beginners' English, and find some excuse for putting the beginners again on Herbert's schedule. But the sub-freshmen give me a splendid chance for letting loose my theories on helpless beings, and I confess that I am vain—or is conceited the word?—enough to like the sensation of handing out knowledge *ex cathedra*.

I am teaching the boys how to plan and construct an essay. Many of my teachers thought they had finished their work when they had given us a subject and corrected the essay. Not so Mrs. G. We began with words. Then came the sentences. Then separate and related paragraphs. We keep juggling with the principles of unity, clearness, and force. Once a week we do a formal essay. I do not simply announce my subject and leave my struggling boy to evolve an atrocious piece of writing. No. I write the subject on the board. Then call for concisely stated facts about it. These facts are numbered and copied by the boys. When we have about twenty facts, we indicate roughly possible combinations. The boys have a clear idea of the difference between a Subject and a Theme. We have forged ahead a bit into the study of the figure of speech (*Mejaz*, as it is called in Turkish). This appeals deeply, because Orientals see and think and speak in figures. They are poets.

I had a whole week of lectures on figures, and now the boys are learning the way to make and recognize the different ones. This has been done entirely without a text-book. I found early in the game that the boys could memorize rapidly. Put this with the fact that they think excellence in scholarship consists in giving you back again what you said. I reversed the old-fashioned way of clearing the decks for action by lining up a lot of stupid and meaningless definitions. Absorb information first, I say; handle it, get acquainted with it, digest it—then, with a background of experience, classify your ideas and concentrate them into definitions.

Later

You lost the chance of your lifetime. Mother. I broke off suddenly the learned lecture on rhetoric. Henri Imer and Herbert were coming in from their ride, and I had literally to jump down the stairs to get the *glacé* fruits out of the way in the kitchen before Herbert would burst in and find them there, spread out all over the room on buttered paper. We are a big family, and I made a lot.

I am thinking of my Christmases. This is the first I have ever spent away from you.

Tarsus, January eighth,
Nineteen-Nine.

It isn't because my husband is brand-new, or that we are living what is supposed to be "that difficult first year" that I object to separations. If this first year is difficult, come on the rest of the years, I say. But I already know, from our engagement days, what separations mean. Still, I saw quite distinctly, when Herbert's father sent him a check to go to the Holy Land, that he ought not to miss the chance. We may not get out this way again. I put it to myself: it will be a glorious thing *to have done!* So I told him he must seize the day. I could not accompany him for a reason that you may guess. I have not told you before: one doesn't always know one's self.

Our holidays and examinations are arranged according to the Oriental Christmases. So they come in January to take in the period from the sixth to the nineteenth. It isn't a long time for a trip: but the Holy Land is not far away. Herbert started off two days ago on the Greek Christmas, and I took Socrates down to Mersina with me to see him off. Being Socrates' Christmas, we could avoid our own lack of gaiety in the last meal by blowing him to a big dinner at the hotel.

You ought to have seen Herbert embarking for Syria, with Mr. Gould, an Englishman on our faculty, and half a dozen boys who live at Alexandretta, the next port—near enough and cheap enough to go home for the holidays. Mr. G. and Herbert took deck passage with the boys. It is January, with snow on the Taurus and cold winds on the Plain, but the Mediterranean blew hot on the day they left, and they could change to a cabin the next day, if it was too cold to spend the second night to Jaffa on deck. Herbert wore an old suit that we intended to throw away, and a black *fez*. With the beard he has grown

19

to make him look older in the classroom, he is for all the world like a Russian pilgrim.

Herbert is to be gone two weeks. Work is an antidote for the "mopes." I tell myself that he may be delayed in returning, and that I may have to tide over the first few days of the new term. So I am working up psychology lectures. I chew over a phrase like William James's "states of consciousness as such" until I fall asleep. I have to begin all over again the next morning, for I cannot remember what he means by "as such."

Dr. Christie knows how to handle women to perfection. We are a small circle, and he says that wives must share in the faculty meetings. He declares that he wants our opinion and our advice, and that "the very best example set to the Orientals is to show them how we respect and defer to our women." But I know this is only half the truth. He takes us in, so that we won't be able to criticize decisions in which we had no part. I knit in faculty meetings. My college education never destroyed the woman's instinct to have hands constantly occupied. Only, I sometimes forget and go ahead at my knitting mechanically. The first baby-band I made in faculty meeting was big enough to go around Herbert. So I called it a cholera belt and gave it to him.

Orientals love to talk and talk and talk and talk. So do Occidentals. And in faculty meetings I have discovered that men are not a bit less garrulous than women. Since I committed matrimony I've found to my surprise that the other sex has very much the same failings as mine. This comes out in faculty meetings. I bet I'd find the same thing in corporation board meetings. Everyone loves to talk, listens impatiently to others when they talk, watches for an opportunity to get another word, and gives in through weariness or indifference rather than through conviction. The best talker has it over the best thinker every time.

Mersina, January eighteenth.

I have written you about the Doughty-Wylies, how they stopped for lunch with us in Tarsus on their way from Konia, the summer British Consulate, to the winter Consulate at Mersina, and what joy it was for us to meet them. A few days later, a letter came with the inscription "For the Youngest Bride at St. Paul's College." It was a weekend invitation for Herbert and me. We went down to Mersina the very next Saturday. That was in October. Since then, weekends with the Doughty-Wylies have been in a certain sense oases—you understand what I mean. The British Consulate means that world of ours which seems far away, and is missed occasionally in spite of the novelty of Tarsus life and the cordiality of the missionaries. At the Doughty-Wylies, I am able to dress in the evening, and Herbert always looks best to me in his dinner-coat. We are unconventional until we get back into convention: then we wonder how and why we ever broke loose.

With tea served when you wake up, ten o'clock help-yourself-when-you-want breakfasts, a morning canter, *siesta* after lunch, and whiskey-and-soda and smokes in the evening—we are thirty miles only from Tarsus, and yet three thousand. We are back in an English country home. We can smell the box and feel the cold and fear the rain—so strong is the influence of the interior—until we step out-of-doors into the sunshine that makes us thankful, after all, that "back in England" was only a dream.

The major is still in his thirties but has had a whole lifetime of adventure crowded into fifteen years of active service in India, Somaliland, Egypt, and South Africa. He has not been robust of late, and was given this consular post temporarily. Intends to return to active army service. Mrs. Doughty-Wylie is a little woman full of life and spirits. She loves nursing—has been after the bubonic plague in India and followed the British Army in the Boer War. Frank and outspoken, you never know what she is going to say next. She is as vehement as the major is mild, as bubbling over as he is cool, as Scotch as he is English. They are lovely to us, and as they have taken on with travel a sense of humour, we have great sessions, sitting around a log-fire until all hours of the night. The major is keen on the Seljuk Turks. He is going to wean Herbert away from French to Ottoman history, I think. Plays up the possibilities of the field for research in glowing terms.

You can imagine how I whooped when Mrs. Doughty-Wylie wrote just after Herbert left that I "really must spend the time your husband is away with us." Socrates was brushing and cleaning Herbert's clothes, and an iron was on to press the trousers. I left them hanging on the line, with caution to Socrates to be sure to take them in that night. Suitcases were quickly packed. I took the next train to Mersina. Wouldn't you have done so to be able to wake the next morning at nine, and have a maid push back the curtains while you sipped tea and munched thin toast? Then, too, I hated everything about our quarters at Tarsus, cosy as they were, with Herbert away.

After a week of a lazy, restful relaxing, just as I was beginning to fall in the frame of mind to wonder how we ever happened to get out into this country and to feel sure that we would never come back, and when I was speculating on the mysterious phenomenon of the best of England's blood content always to live away from home, Herbert returned. I woke up one morning, and there he stood in the room, looking down at me. He declared that ten days in the Holy Land—without me—was enough for him. He had "done" Jerusalem and bathed in the Dead Sea—but Galilee could wait for another time. There was a swift Italian steamer up the coast. He saw it posted at Cook's in Jerusalem. Hurried down to Jaffa and caught it. We have decided that separations are not a success. May there be no more. As we do not have to go back to Tarsus for two days, we are staying on to pass Armenian Christmas with the Doughty-Wylies. They are going to take us pig-sticking tomorrow.

Tarsus,
January twenty-second.

Today we rode across the Plain to the Cave of the Seven Sleepers. I enjoy "training the Turks." They let their wives walk while they ride. Sometimes the poor woman will have a child or some other load on her back. You can imagine they do not turn aside to give a woman the path, not even a foreign lady. Sometimes I jar their sensibilities by standing my horse sturdily in their path. It never enters their head that I do not intend to turn out. When I rein up with the nose of my horse right in their face (they are generally on little donkeys) they have an awful shock. Reluctantly they give way to me, always looking injured and surprised. Sometimes they express their feeling in language that I fortunately cannot understand. I love to speak to them in English. I say something like this: "You old unwashed villain, I am sure you haven't used Pears' or any other soap this or any other morning. Hurry up, and get out of my way."

We came across a donkey standing patiently by the roadside. His halter-rope was tied around the leg of his rider, a boy who lay moaning on the grass. We had Socrates ask him in Turkish what the matter was. He responded that he had a fever and was too ill to go on. Herbert told Socrates to set the boy on his donkey. He went several miles with us, groaning all the way. We encouraged him, and fortunately soon met some people from his village. The Turks are absolutely indifferent to human suffering, and would have let him die there like a dog. Outside of large centres of population, they have no physicians, no hospitals, no medicines—it is only through the missionaries that such things are known at all. At last we reached our mountain-goal, and climbed up to the cave. The *mullah* received us cordially. Turks are polite and hospitable to travellers. I will say that for them. The *mullah's* servant stabled our horses, brought us water, and allowed us to spread our lunch on the front porch of the mosque. It is a pretty little mosque, and right beside it is a home for the *mullah* built of stone. Both are close to the entrance of the cave. The group of buildings looked beautiful from the bottom of the hill. But as is invariably the case in Turkey, close inspection revealed the primitiveness and roughness.

After lunch, during which the servant and his little boy gravely sat and watched us, we went into the cave. We took our shoes off against our will, for the cave looked dirty and mussy. Down a long flight of stone steps the beturbaned guardian led us into a sickening atmosphere of incense and goatskin. We were told that the cave was large, but, as we were in stocking feet and had noses, we elected not to explore it. During the Decian persecutions, seven young men fled from Tarsus to this cave to escape. Here they fell asleep. They were miraculously kept asleep for one hundred years. Waking they thought it was the next day, and went down to a nearby village. They were surprised to learn that the whole world was Christian. This is the genesis, or at least the Oriental version, of the Rip Van Winkle story. The Christians built a shrine at the cave. The invading Mohammedan conquerors took it over and adapted shrine and legend to their own religion, as they have done with most Christian holy places.

We sketched the mosque in the afternoon. Then we sat looking out over the plain to the sea. It is great to have a chance to talk to one's husband. We are so busy during the week that we save up our talks for Saturday and Sunday, and we are just getting to know each other. The keeper told us through Socrates that his wife had died seven years before and that he lived there all alone, except for the *mullah*, with his little five year old boy. The kid sang a song for us. We gave him slices of bread thickly spread with jam, which he ate with gusto. It was probably the first jam he had ever tasted—certainly the first Crosse & Blackwell's strawberry jam.

After the feast was over, he crept up slyly, seized Herbert's hand, and imprinted on it a sticky kiss. We were saddled and ready to start homeward immediately after tea, but not soon enough to get away from the hail-storm that came up all of a sudden. Before we were out of the stable, the storm broke, great big hailstones that stung when they hit you. We rode hard for twenty minutes, enjoying it keenly. It rained just long enough to make the sunset richer and the air sweeter than usual. We do not mind a bit getting wet like that when we are on horse. By riding fast, the wind soon dries our outer garments and the rain does not penetrate. By the time we reached home, we were dry and did not need to change our clothes before dinner. After our exercise a good warm bath made us sleep like the pair of healthy children we are.

CHAPTER 3

A Visit to Adana

Adana,
February eighteenth.

Dearest Mother:

You know how I love weekend visits. I used to put Uncle John's Christmas cheque into a hundred-trip ticket between Bryn Mawr and Philadelphia: so that if my allowance ran low I could get away from college over Sunday anyway.

Weekend visits here are really not had at all. There is no hotel in this town. Characteristically, Daddy Christie has the office force at the station pilot foreigners coming to Tarsus straight to St. Paul's College, no matter what orders they gave. A variety of folks wash up on our beach. A dignified professor with a little group of Oxford men bound for the interior to prove on the ground that there are villages back in the Taurus where ancient Greek persists unadulterated to this day, came back a few weeks later, faces beaming with the grin research scholars wear when they have it on the other authorities. Another group of men said they were travellers. Americans of the Far West they certainly were.

We couldn't make out much else at first. Their leader sat next to me at lunch, and was so extraordinarily reticent, when, in trying to make conversation, I asked him about his family, that I commented upon it afterwards to Herbert and Dr. Christie. Later we learned that they were Mormon missionaries. Dear Dr. Deissmann, with others from the University of Berlin, spent two days with us on their journey in the footsteps of Saint Paul. He is gathering material for a book that will make a stir in the world. He spoke before the boys, in excellent English—what linguists Germans are!—and the college orchestra responded with *Die Wacht am Rhein*. It was a *noble* effort, and the *Herr*

Professor was good enough to beam and applaud.

Weekends would indeed be dull were it not for visits exchanged up and down the railway by missionaries in Mersina, Tarsus and Adana. A new person at any of the three stations is very soon invited to make weekend visits. Early in the autumn, Miss X arrived at Adana. When she made her first visit to Tarsus, Herbert and I invited her to have coffee in our study one Saturday evening. Kind of cosy, sitting in front of our fire, and she loosened up and told us that there was just one thing that troubled her in Adana. That was the Swiss teacher of French at the Girls' Boarding School, who said she was much relieved to find that the newcomer understood a little French, "Because, my dear, it is important for me to safeguard my English. You see I cannot risk catching your American accent."

Mother, I was mad as a hornet, and what I did proves that I am no good as a missionary. We told Miss X that when this petty persecution was being carried on, she was to be like B'rer Rabbit, and *"jes' keep on sayin' nothin'."*

When the Swiss teacher came for a weekend, we invited her for coffee. As she settled herself before our fire, she said engagingly: "Now you must speak French with me. Take every chance you can for practice."

"Thank you, *Mademoiselle*," I answered, "we should rather speak English. We are going to live in Paris, you know, and don't dare risk catching your Swiss accent."

No, Mother dear, that wasn't like a missionary, was it? I am not sorry I said it. When I went to Adana, Miss X told me that the teasing had suddenly ceased after *mademoiselle's* Tarsus visit.

Mrs. Nesbit Chambers invited me to spend a whole week with her. Herbert was to come over the following Sunday to bring me home. The train conductor who speaks passable French gave up to me his own private compartment. Some weeks since, I should have been aghast at the thought of going off all alone in Turkey and in Asia on such a queer train, with outlandish fellow travellers, to a place where I had never been. But things become familiar to one in a very short time. It seemed almost as natural as South Station, Broad Street, Grand Central, Trenton, Princeton, New Haven, Annapolis or Bryn Mawr—a year ago my whole world.

After the train pulled out of Tarsus, I felt that I had my nerve with me. But I was too interested in what I saw from the window to occupy my mind regretting that I had not waited until Herbert could come with me. The uncle of Krikor Effendi's bride (I mean the conductor) was most polite, and left me alone in his reserved compartment. At the first station an old brigand got off with a brilliant red tangled rug on his shoulder. I recognized it as the Cretan rug we had been bargaining for. Evidently he had not been able to get his price in Tarsus. A Turk on horse came up to meet the train. The horse jumped around so that his saddle turned. The man fell off safely, but his friends were still struggling to turn the saddle straight when we tooted on. At another station, a shiny tinned trunk, just like a big doll's trunk made in Germany, was dumped off. Two husky Kurds picked it up, and carried it to a turbaned Hodja on a tall white horse, who put the trunk in front of him on the saddle, and started off at a run across the plain. After an hour I became cold, and was glad I had my steamer rug.

At Adana, a polite individual asked me whether he could find a carriage for me. I told him Mrs. Chambers would come. He said to wait right there. I stood on the platform in the midst of the most variegated crowd I had ever seen—even in the Tarsus bazaars. The whole town was either getting off the train or had come to meet friends. Some day the Bagdad Railway will go on from here. But now this is the terminus of the line from Mersina, and there is none yet across the Taurus to Konia.

I was glad to see Mrs. Chambers coming. We rode up to her house in an open carriage. I did not want the top up, in spite of the cold. It was all so new and strange to me. The *arabadjis* (drivers) in Turkey are sons of Jehu. Carriages are the only things I have found yet that move fast. You cannot help being nervous about running people down. It never happens, though.

When I was once indoors I had no desire to take off my sweater or my long coat. My nose and ears were as numb as fingers and toes. Mrs. Chambers gave me two cups of hot tea and I felt better. She took me into her guest room, and cautioned me to be careful about the bedspread. "I keep it for special people," she explained, "like the British Consul's wife and you. But that is no reason why either of you should fail to be careful of it, for it is the best thing I have." The crockery washstand took my eye. It was dark green from basin to tooth-mug.

During the few minutes before supper we climbed up on the roof for the red winter sunset. The Chamberses live in the heart of the Armenian quarter on the top of the hill. Quite a change after flat Tarsus. The Armenians have to go to the river to get their water. What a back-breaking job for the women! They carry tall jars on their shoulders. We could see the mountains behind Alexandretta in Syria very plainly. There was snow on the summits.

Adana,
February twenty-second.

The Girls' School of the Mission is run by women-folks. I went over there for a meal, and had a look at the teachers and the pupils. When I saw the girls all collected in the schoolroom, they seemed to me infinitely pathetic. They are mostly Armenians. In spite of the curves and glow and bloom of their youth, they look like little women. Perhaps it is because of the sadness that lurks in their eyes. What chance have girls in this country anyway? Ought we not to wait until the country is changed politically before we bring them up to live in our sort of a world?

In Tarsus the houses are mostly of stone, because the moderns have used the remains right at hand for successive rebuilding through centuries. The ancient city, in Roman Imperial days, was so large that it is an inexhaustible quarry. Modern Adana, on the other hand, is much larger than the ancient city, and Roman stone gave out long ago. You never hear of the Turks going to the trouble of stone-cutting. Where they are not able to utilize the labour of past ages, they build for the day. Consequently, Adana is a city of wood, totally unlike Tarsus. This, with the hill, and the big river right in the town, makes Adana more picturesque. The background of mountains and rich plain is the same, however. Turkish wooden houses are built haphazard, with no idea of architecture, and they are never repaired.

All except the new ones look as if they were just about to fall down. Many are falling down. Holes are patched with new boards or more frequently with flattened-out petroleum tins. Balconies are stayed with props. When the inevitable day of collapse arrives, the Turks thank *Allah* that the catastrophe did not happen sooner, and praise *Allah's* mercy in giving them firewood for next winter. A mass of wooden houses in Turkey makes an *ensemble* of brown, of different shades, depending upon the age of the house. The Turks do not paint: for they calculate that a house will last at least as long as the man who built it. The next generation can look after itself.

Oriental houses are reticent, like the women who live in them. They are meant for animals and women, the animals on the ground floor and the women upstairs—both created and kept in captivity to work for man. You can tell a Christian from a Moslem house from the fact that the Moslems put lattice-work over the windows. Otherwise they are the same. While Christians do not seclude their women, they have nearly the same ideas about making them work.

Miss Hallie Wallis has her home and dispensary near the Girls' School, in a house built with a blind wall toward the street, and windows opening only on the court. Within the court an outside stairway, mounting to the balcony, leads to the living part of the house. When I went to call, I got into the hospital side. Miss Wallis popped out of her office to receive me and led me into a waiting-room which, although furnished only with a few carpets and divans sporting wide-meshed native crochet tidies, was cosy. At the door were the patients' wooden clogs. In one corner a soft-voiced Armenian Bible woman was talking with an elderly blind woman and a little blind boy. These people were in their stocking feet, and although I knew it was the native custom, I felt that they had left their clogs at the door out of respect to Miss Hallie's spotless rooms. Miss Wallis gently divined fatigue that I didn't know was there. In a few minutes, although it was mid-morning, there was a steaming cup of tea and the paper-thin slices of bread and butter that can be made only by an Englishwoman.

The Armenian doctor asked me to take a look at the work. He gave me a high stool near his operating table. The hours of the morning flew as I watched the tender skilful handling of the cases, one after another. This is the only real medical care the people of Adana receive—and it is a city of sixty thousand! I saw eighty-seven people come and go. Of these fifty-eight were eye cases. Miss Wallis has books for the blind, and a Bible woman who does nothing else but read to them. She is a thorough-going saint, this Miss Wallis, a gentle, tireless saint. How many women there are in the world, women of means, of brains and position, who, in unawakened stolidity, live wasted lives! They belong to the army of the unemployed just as much as bums and hoboes.

Some unmarried women, middle-aged ones, feel a little bitter as they look upon their married sisters' lives. That is because they are not working. Here is a woman who, by self-abnegation and glad assumption of responsibility, has the richness of life and the wide full satisfaction a mother feels in doing for her brood of children. Mothers haven't really a corner on contentment and blessedness. The most common examples of unselfishness and happiness that we see about us are the mothers. But there is opportunity for all women to become happy through service, and thus taste the joy of motherhood. Think of the many unmothered people in the world, both kids and grown-ups, that cry out for woman-souls to shelter and minister to them.

When we finished the morning's work in the clinic, Miss Wallis went with me to lunch at Mrs. Chambers'. As we walked along the street, a haggard old woman stopped us, clutching at a fold of Miss Wallis's coat. "Please tell me," came the rapid question, "why you are so happy? I have seen people who looked as happy as you do, but never before two women each one happier than the other. Can you tell me why? Are you sisters?"

"Yes, yes," said Miss Wallis, "we are sisters. God is love, *Madama* and you and I are his children, and so we are sisters." Miss Wallis stopped right there to explain further. Before we went on our way the old woman heard the Good News the missionaries come here to tell, and she hobbled away happy because she was a sister to somebody who was happy.

I fell in love with the green pitcher and basin in my bedroom. Mrs. Chambers took me to the pottery. In a cellar, without much light, the potter was working at his wheel. He was making an amphora of the common kind women and donkeys carry to the fountains. His right arm was inside the jar. He worked the wheel with his foot, and with his left hand guided the rude uneven course of the paddle-like affair which was moulding a lump of clay into shape. With the very slightest pressure, the potter was able to change radically the contour of the clay. It was the first time I had ever seen the potter and the wheel. I understood.

In the courtyard was a scrap heap piled high with all sorts of broken and rain-soaked bits of discarded vessels. I spotted a little squat vase, just my colour of green. You know the soft shade the underside of apple leaves take on when you lie in a hammock under the apple-tree and half close your eyes as you look up at the sky on a cloudy day in spring. Kicking aside the debris with my foot, I pulled out the vase by its uncovered handle. The other handle was safe. Rough lines, grooved by the potter's will, had dried into the lovely thing before it was polished, and the glaze added by the fire must have been weather-worn in this old courtyard for more years than I am old. There was a slight depression, left by the potter's thumb, on the bottom of the vase. A police magistrate could have made a thumb-print from it. I bought the vase for two cents. It is my most precious possession.

CHAPTER 4

Great Expectations

Tarsus, March fifteenth,
Nineteen-Nine,

Dearest Mother:

Do you remember the day I was talking to you about the mother-in-law problem and I said I was put to it to know what to call her? You said, "Don't worry, it won't be long before you have somebody to whom she will be grandma, and you can get out of it gracefully by calling her grandma, too." Isn't it queer to think that I through my motherhood shall place you in the grandmother generation? As I look back to Cloverton days and my grandmother, I envy this baby of mine. There is something about a grandmother that is pretty fine. They thought I was a great kid at grandma's house—partly because of my unshakable belief that my grandmother was beautiful. How I used to stand beside her chair stroking her cheek, telling her, "You are beautiful." She used to smile with her eyes while her lips protested, saying, "How can I be beautiful with all my wrinkles?" I suppose it was the Irish coming out in me: for I remember distinctly telling her that she had no wrinkles, except pretty laugh wrinkles on both sides of her eyes.

Don't hug secret reflections about growing old. When you and I and the grandbaby meet *it* will be Helen's responsibility. You will be free to play with the baby. That has not happened to you since you were a little girl and had dolls. I shall say: "Oh, Mother is there, so baby is safe." The meeting of the three generations will eliminate worry. Nature means young fathers and mothers and babies to have grandmother near. You must come to Paris next winter.

You have made a jolly start in grandmotherhood. It was better than Christmas, when Daddy Christie and Herbert opened your box.

I have my small steamer trunk right beside our wardrobe, and am playing it is the baby hamper. The trunk is nearly brand new, and will do very well when we leave here in June, for it will hold all the baby things.

★★★★★★

A perfume can whisk your mind five thousand miles from your body. I am sitting beside our white iron bed, sniffing. There is the faint unfamiliar odour given out by my cedar woodwork, the smell of fresh whitewash on new walls, the warm breath of a log fire. Dominating it all is the clean clover sachet you sprinkled among the baby clothes. The sachet carried my memory straight back to home, for it smells like your upper bureau drawer.

The baby things came this morning, and I have arranged them on the bed, so that when Herbert comes back from teaching his Greek class, he will get the full benefit. Dresses and petticoats, silk-and-wool shirts and bands, didies—all six months size. Do you fear that I will not be able to nurse your grandbaby, that you sent all the condensed and malted milk?

Next time you have to go to Doctor Smith's office, give him my thanks for his kind message. I can hear him gravely telling you to advise me "by all means to go to the nearest hospital." Take with you my old geography, and put your pretty forefinger on the right-hand upper corner of the Mediterranean. Show him that we are where the map begins to turn around that right-hand upper corner down towards the Holy Land. Then tell him the nearest hospital is a two days' sea voyage away. Do you suppose Herbert's salary could send me to Beirut? And could I take the journey alone?

You are quite justified, however, in your wish that I make plans now for baby's coming. The only trained nurse in Cilicia is Miss Hallie Wallis. She is forty miles away. She receives at her house at least one hundred natives a day and has more work than her limited strength can accomplish. Moreover, she has such a mixed crowd that it might not be wise for her to handle a baby case.

If we had taken the little church in Squeedunkville we used to talk about in Princeton days, instead of setting out to see the world like a couple of fellows in a Grimm's fairy tale, you would now be forwarding the bassinette Grandma gave me when I was born. Some nosey old parishioner would be trimming it up for me. I am a Presbyterian, turned Congregationalist on account of geography, but "conformity unto" would give me fits when it came to parishioners' notions. I am

32

much too hasty and human to suit anybody.

Your grandbaby will open its eyes five thousand miles from its grandmother. The family heirlooms must wait for the second grandbaby.

Some weeks ago I had the school steward (name, when spoken, sounds like Asturah) go to a Fellahin village near Tarsus and have a basket made for me. A Fellahin village itself looks like a dusty unfinished basket turned upside down. The houses are made of a crude reed matting, and the side walls have the reeds untrimmed and upright at the place where you expect to see eaves.

I figured out the size for my cradle basket, then cut strings of the right length for the various dimensions. Through an interpreter I explained that the basket must be oval. As wide at the top as my blue string, as wide at the bottom as my red string and as deep as my white string. A week later the basket was brought to our balcony. Herbert and I climbed into the thing. It was big enough for us to sit down in it Turkish fashion, both at the same time.

I got my cradle finally "by some ingenious method." (One of the students is always saying that.) Funny how the boys here pick out bookish expressions and use them for everything. I collected my strings again, suspecting that they had not been out of Asturah's belt pocket since the day I gave them to him. You ought to see those belts! The natives take a square of wool material with a striped blue and brown and red Persian design, fold it corner-wise, and attach one end to their potato-sack trousers. Then they wind this affair around and around their middle and fasten it on the other side. The shawl is pretty big to begin with. They keep an amazing number and variety of things in the fold of this belt; dagger, package of bread and cheese and olives for lunch, and a little brass contrivance for holding pen and ink. There is really some sense to this kind of a belt in a blow-cold, blow-hot country, for it keeps tummies warm and protects from intestinal troubles. No wonder natives get along without expensive Jaeger cholera belts.

This time I sent Socrates with my strings to the tinsmith in the bazaar. He made me a tin affair according to my measurements. Baby's bathtub. Next I sent the bathtub to the Fellahin with orders to make a basket covering for it, the same shape as the "tin dish" to protect it during a long journey we expected soon to take. The weaver then had in his mind's eye just how tub and basket would be strapped on one side of a pack-saddle. For these people, a journey means going somewhere on horseback. When we sail for Marseilles in June, I will put the tub into the basket, pillows, didies and mattress into the tub, cover the whole with a Turkish cradle shawl we bought yesterday, and fasten it with a big strap. The cradle shawl is two yards square, made of coarse woollen material. If you please, it is dyed brilliant red and green, with alternating checks. How is that for something dainty for a baby?

In the middle of the shawl, about a yard apart, are round button-holes. One is worked in green and the other red. A native mother would hitch these buttonholes to little pegs that stand up at either end of the box-like affair she uses for a cradle to protect the baby inside from fresh air. Germs are carefully tucked into the cradle with the baby. Never mind, I am going to give my cradle shawl a good cleaning, and I expect it will serve me well as outer covering for the package I shall make of the tub and bed and bedding. I must plan thoughtfully for that journey. It will be worthwhile to do this because we have to go to Egypt in order to get a good boat for Marseilles and that makes a twelve-day voyage.

Cotton crops are coming in. I bought a pile, and had a man fluff it up with a stringed instrument that looks for all the world like a giant's violin bow. On the first windless day I put it on a sheet, spread out in the tennis court, for a day's sunshine. The sunshine here reminds me of Nice at its best.

In the bazaar I bought white material, something like *piqué*. When I washed and ironed it, I cut out two oval pieces a little larger than the bottom of the basket, joined the two ovals with a band five inches wide, stuffed this with the cotton,—and behold a jolly little mat-tress! Lucky thing I am so attached to those two wee pillows I had at college. Lucky, too, that I bought a new set of pillow cases for them before I left home. After I find suitable material and make a pair of blankets, my cradle will be ready. When the Queen of Holland's baby comes, it won't find a better bed.

We have been laughing at Daddy and Mother Christie. One night there was chicken for dinner, and by accident not quite enough to go around. Daddy fussed and made jokes, and we soon forgot all about it. Not so Daddy. He went to the bazaar, and came home with the announcement that he had bought one hundred chickens. Boys were hastily put to work to make a pen, and fenced off a run! The chickens arrived that same afternoon, and Daddy laid down the law to the two chaps who were to take care of them. He said his chickens would cost the school nothing. He was paying for them out of his Civil War pension. The chickens were photographed. Dr. Christie had a lot of prints made and sent to America. On the back of each photograph he wrote: "The lay workers of Tarsus." Now he has the laugh on all of us. The photographs and Daddy's inscription have already brought in much more money in gifts to the college than the chickens and photographs and postage cost. Typical! Such a darling he is. He looks like Carnegie. If he had Carnegie's fortune, we should have to call him Daddy Christmas.

This is a great life. We may have evil-tasting fat made of melted-down sheep-tails, and no butter for our bread, but there are bowls of thirst-quenching bonny-clabber and rolled pats of buffalo cream. The rice may be half-cooked, and the bread may taste sour, but almost any day I can send to the kitchen where the students' food is prepared and get a plate of *bulgur* made of coarse ground wheat. We have fresh figs stewed or raw and honeysweet, and oh, the oranges. I am guilty of one "notion." I eat quantities of these golden oranges, about fourteen a day. I may feel the limitations of life in Turkey in many ways, but until I outgrow them, I can put on my khaki riding things, swing into my Mexican saddle and at sunset ride like the wind across the Cilician Plain with the crying of jackals and the chant of the *muezzins* in my ears. The law of compensation is a fact, my dear, and let me tell you this—don't feel sorry for missionaries.

CHAPTER 5

Round About Tarsus

April fourth, Nineteen-Nine.

Dearest Mother:

I haven't written since I told you the biggest news a girl can give her mother, and then I was so full of it that I did not answer the questions your letters have been reiterating for many months. What is Tarsus like? What sort are the people, and your school boys? What do you and Herbert do with yourselves out there in that God-forsaken country? It is precisely because we have been trying to find out all about Tarsus and get to know the people and the boys that I have neglected writing. That is part of the reason. The biggest part has to do with horses. You know how we love to ride—and here we have learned what it really means to ride. It isn't a genteel afternoon tea parade through a park where everyone you meet is as sick of seeing you and the park as you are sick of seeing them and the park. When conventional city folk look at a bird or an animal in a cage, and are sorry for the poor thing, it is only another sign of lack of realisation as well as of imagination. With my teas and balls and clothes I was blissfully happy at home: but so was our canary. Neither of us knew any better, for we knew only our prison.

We have been round about Tarsus everywhere, and every day, rain or shine. There is very little of the former. From the moment of our arrival in Mersina last August, aside from an hour or so in the morning of tennis, and an occasional visit to the bazaars, all our out-of-doors has been on horse. We have explored the city and the neighbourhood, and have tried the roads on the Plain in every direction. Herbert's sky-piloting in Idaho gave him a taste for restless stallion mounts, and I encourage it. Mastering horses is training for mastering men. There is nothing in the world better for the teacher than to ride high-spirited horses. The other day we took out a new horse Henri Imer is thinking of buying. We had him from a villager, who declared the horse was in a town for the first time. It was true! For he shied at every little thing. I tried him first, and had great fun making him go through crowded streets and the bazaars. The noise in the copper and tin bazaar drove him wild. But I had him in hand: for Turkish bits give you the hold. He did not like the butcher stalls. Such a time. It cost me ten *piastres* to the indignant butcher to get the better of the horse. But I did it by making him go straight up and rub his nose in freshly-cut pot-roasts. There was no danger for pedestrians. In Turkey the people are used to camels and horses and buffaloes "acting regardless." Pedestrians know how to get out of the way.

Coming home, Herbert was trying the fractious beast. We took him around by a water-wheel which we call the "third degree." It is our final stunt in town-breaking a village horse. The water-wheel stands almost at right-angles with the road. Its little buckets dip up the water and empty some ten feet above into an irrigation trench. The hub of the wheel screeches and the buckets keep up a clank-clank, accompanied by a thud as they go into the water and a sucking sound as they come out. The road is narrow—brook on one side and wall on the other. Over the wall protrude branches of a tree, wrapped round by hanging vines. It is low bridge for fair. Herbert, leaning over the neck of the frightened beast, had all kinds of trouble. We knew the animal had no intention of falling into the stream. Horses don't. The horse, however, refused to pass the wheel. Each time he backed Pony and me some yards down the road. Finally Herbert lost his whip. It fell into the stream. Herbert looked relieved. But you know, Mother, the elemental in me would not allow me to see a horse get the better of my man. I gave Herbert my whip. He tried again, and got by. Pony, who had long ago received "the third degree" when we first discovered that wheel, followed easily.

Alas, the days of horseback have passed for me until next summer.

The other day we made a second trip to the sea, this time in a carriage. Socrates was on the box, and Herbert was gallant enough to forego his mount and ride with me.

Halfway we stopped at a *tchiflik* (farmhouse) to water the horses and try to buy eggs. Every farmer has half a dozen dogs—ugly fellows that give low growls. They hate you the way their Mohammedan masters hate you. After the tenant of the farmhouse had driven back his dogs, he surprised us by showing unusual friendliness. We asked for eggs. He said he had none. This we knew was cheerful mendacity: so we pressed him further. Finally he brought us a whole basket of eggs, saying that he ought not to sell them, because he was supposed to send them all to the town to Pasha Somebody or Other. As we were leaving, we put a coin into his hand. He would not take it! Socrates gave it to a little girl who was apparently the child of the tenant. Some superstition made the father hesitate to take the money directly from us. Farther along, a lone dead tree twisted itself above the masonry of a typical oriental well of ancient origin.

As we stopped our carriage a moment, we saw a solitary owl sitting motionless on a loosened stone. When we drove on, the owl turned his head slowly following us, like a spirit of a forgotten century resenting with superb unconcern the investigating energy of modern times. A flock, no, I ought to call it a whole nation, of wild geese was quietly standing, undisturbed by our approach and arranged in little groups as if according to tribes, although all were facing the same way. They looked like the men of different counties in the same state—drawn up in military line and waiting for orders. Herbert and Socrates growled because they had no guns with them. I was glad that such perfect unity did not have to be broken up just to amuse us.

When we reached the sea the old gray horse wanted to have another roll in the sand. The last time he had seen the sand was the day he tried to roll with me on his back. Socrates unhitched the horses, and soon it was time for luncheon. We settled ourselves on steamer rugs and unpacked our provisions. We had tea made in my tea-basket and cold turkey, the remains of Sunday dinner. When lunch was finished, Herbert and I took a long walk on the beach. It was a blustery day when sunshine alternates with low swiftly-moving clouds. Ahead of us was the town of Mersina, a curved line of mingled flat roofs and slender minarets. A mile out to sea lay half a dozen ships, and we knew that there must be mail for us in Mersina.

After we turned back towards the place where our camp was, we could see beyond it a ramshackle structure, lonely and abandoned now—since the New Constitution. Here used to be stationed a guard—not a Life Saving Guard, such as we should have in a similar place—a guard whose whole duty it was to watch for Armenians, who chose this part of the seashore to escape in small boats. From here it was comparatively easy to get a ship and go away from Turkey forever. There was romance, as well as adventure, in these escapes. A young Armenian found means to go to America, and there made plenty of money. Back here on this Cilician Plain a girl was waiting. The man saved up enough to come back and get the girl. His friends smuggled her out to the ship, a missionary was pressed into service, and a wedding at sea took place. The bride and groom sailed away, returning to New York or Chicago, to live happily ever afterwards. You see the young man had become an American citizen. If he landed on Turkish soil, the new citizenship would have been lost. That is why his bride had to go out to the ship to be married. The guardhouse must have frequently intercepted such weddings: for it is built where it commands the coast Mersinawards.

On the way home we saw a great deal of black smoke. This meant some people were having fun driving wild boar out of the swamps. You get natives for "beaters," build fires through the canebrake, and then you wait patiently. There is sure to be a reward if your "beaters" don't take the stick or the shot before you get your spear or your gun ready. The last time we were visiting the British Consul in Mersina, the Doughty-Wylies took us pig-sticking. After making elaborate arrangements, with any number of native "beaters" in tow, the best shot of the day was lost just this way. The "beaters" did not remember that their job was to beat—not to steal shots they were paid to let slip.

It began to rain. But we didn't care. It was a slanting rain and fortunately dashed against the back of the carriage. We had rugs and coats: so the rain was an addition to the fun. We were careful to protect our driftwood, of which we had gathered enough to make two or three glorious fires. That evening we burned the driftwood, only to be disappointed. Of wonderful colours we got not one flicker. Is this another superstition disproved?

When Herbert writes the letter about Tarsus that he has long been talking about, but never gets down to, he will probably say much about the bazaars. But I am now going to anticipate him. Why not? I have only the typewriter to console me for having to give up my horse. Anyway, we may get away from here and into other things before Herbert tackles Tarsus. I am still waiting to see his letter on the trip he took to the Holy Land.[1]

There are very few women in the bazaars. None at all are engaged in selling. Turkish ladies never go. Rarely one sees Armenian and Fellahin women buying. When the time came to get Christmas gifts for

---

1. More than seven years have passed, and neither the Tarsus letter nor the Holy Land letter has yet been written. Our life moves so fast, in the midst of a great and changing drama, that the event at hand demands all there is of time and energy.

Herbert, I did the markets with one of the seniors. It is perfectly proper for me to go to the bazaars. Foreign women are a different order of beings, absolutely beyond the comprehension of the natives. They look at me as if I had dropped from Mars. I suppose they consider me a sexless being, resembling their women only in the lack of a soul. Menfolks in Turkey, you know, have a corner on souls. Herbert and I have a great deal of fun as we walk about Tarsus.

But I was telling you about my Christmas shopping. I took Harutun, my senior, to the markets half a dozen times. You cannot go to a shop and select the thing you want, then ask the price and have it sent home. Oh, no! You go, and appear to be looking at something else, and let your attention be attracted to the thing you really want—by merest chance. Even then you do not mention this to the merchant. You simply say to your English-speaking boy: "See that little brass bowl in the opposite corner of the shop? I will give him eight *piastres* for it."

Boy says: "Yes, Mrs. Gibbons," and you turn up your nose a little higher as the merchant urges upon you the purchase of some other thing you do not intend to buy. You draw yourself up to your full majestic height, incline your head backward the least little bit, raise your hand in a queenly waving aside, give a little click with your tongue, perhaps emphasizing it by exclaiming in good Turkish: "*Yok*" (which being interpreted means "nothing doing, old man"), and then you indifferently withdraw, followed by your boy. Next day Harutun sends another boy, who gets your brass bowl for about one-quarter the price you'd paid if you had insisted on buying it yourself. That is how shopping is done in the Orient.

In this way I got Herbert a fine old copper tray and a queer pitcher-like thing to go with it. I found two coins whose owner did not appreciate them, and these I had made into a pair of cuff-links. A tiny silver cup, about an inch and a half in diameter, with the dearest little carved handle, was the best thing of all. We use it on our desk as a place to keep pens. I pursued a camel-train, and after a great deal of intrigue came into possession of several camel-bells. These are especially interesting to us because they were bought right off the camel. It reminded me of pigtail days in the Engadine, when I followed a pretty cow home to her owner's chalet, and bought the bell on her neck. Tarsus markets are cosmopolitan. You can find a dozen races rubbing elbows there. The predominating four are Turks, Arab Fellahin, Armenians and Greeks. There is a babel of these four tongues.

One hears also Russian, Persian, Hindustani and Italian. We manage with French in Mersina, but it is little spoken in Tarsus. The Turkish language rules in inter-racial transactions. Armenians must use this language. Educated Armenians struggle valiantly to maintain the two surviving elements of national identity: the church and the language. But oddly enough the mother-tongue of the average Armenian is Turkish. Greek has a strong hold upon the Greeks here. It is something like the tenacious hold of the French language in Canada. The Fellahin speak a form of Arabic, but are too ignorant to care whether they make themselves understood or not. Some weeks ago Jeanne Imer and I were being carefully escorted through a Fellahin village by one of the students. Suddenly a little boy ran into the road. He took hold of my bridle, looked up at me with a winning smile, and said: "From where you come? From America?"

Imagine my surprise. I was delighted to hear my own language away off here in the outskirts of the town. I reached into my coat pocket, pulled out an orange, and gave it to the little fellow. He said "Thank you" most politely. I found afterwards that there is a mission school in the quarter of Tarsus nearest where these people live. The child was evidently a pupil. But wasn't it cute of him to spot me for an American!

Today my rooms are getting an extra house-cleaning, and I have two boys hard at work. One is washing three of my rugs. He has, as little Cousin Myers used to say, "his bare feet on." He jumps up and down on the wet, soapy rugs; then pounds them with a big flat stick that looks like a cricket-bat. They are certainly getting clean—though I doubt whether you and I should adopt that method if we had the job. The boys are trying to talk Armenian to each other. They try hard. But they cannot help falling into Turkish. For in this part of Turkey their mother-tongue is the language of their oppressors—the badge of servitude.

Armenians of breeding and education foster their language with all their heart and soul. There is a desperate attempt to preserve the national unity, always with the opposition of the terrible Turks! The Armenians have natural ability along the line of enterprise and making money, but this has been so curbed by the oppressor that even stout hearts have given up and lapsed into a paralysis of the will that would be contemptible if one did not understand it. Under favourable circumstances, when the Armenian has been given a square deal, he is successful. He is a born merchant. This is proved when he goes to another country where his enterprise can have its own way.

We met a fine young fellow in Adana not long ago. He had come home to see about the education of a little sister in the mission school in Adana. He was in America only six years, but has come back thoroughly Americanized, with a lot of money earned as a candy drummer. He is a good example of our young American hustler who is almost blatantly successful. It was refreshing to meet him, for he sounded like home. The appearance of such a man among his old associates causes considerable dissatisfaction, for he has made more money in this short time than his cousins and brothers can make in a lifetime. The educators of Armenian boys have a problem before them. Are they going to educate the boys in order to encourage them to go to America? Isn't the reason for having the schools to help these people to a better life in their own country? Why educate the bright boys at all, if it is not to equip them to spend their lives for the good of their countrymen?

Yet, what can you answer to the pathetic and conclusive argument that the educated Armenian has no chance for advancement, so long as Armenia is under Turkish rule? They really have no chance, the boys with a diploma. They are educated for unhappiness and for danger. We cannot shut our eyes to the fact that after they have been years in our schools, American education fits them for American opportunities, and unfits them for Turkish opportunities. More than this, after we have given them the vision of another kind of national as well as another kind of individual life, they are marked men among the Turks, and are the first to be sought out when a massacre comes. Herbert and I have our misgivings about all this work here. In spite of the heralded liberty of the constitution, it requires more optimism than we have to believe that Armenians are safer under Young Turks than they were under old Turks. *Bairam* means feast.

After every religious fast, a *bairam*. It is an occasion for eating immoderately, and for giving a little pleasure and break in the dull monotony of woman and child life. During the last *bairam*, in the field of the camel market there was a funny little "merry-go-round" and a crude Ferris wheel, which had hanging wooden cages each big enough to hold four children—if they were small. A beaming brown-faced peasant was taking in the money and bossing the two men who turned the wheel and the merry-go-round. He came up to us, and with real pride in his voice, asked: "Have you anything like this in America?"

On Sunday morning, the classes have their lesson taught in their class-rooms, and then they come together in the assembly-room for the concluding exercises. As these are given in Turkish, Herbert and I do not feel called upon to go. So we commit the heresy of slipping out for a walk. It is a heresy. Mother, to these dear good people.

The missionaries have puritanical notions of Sabbath-keeping that are different from anything Herbert and I have ever run across. Of course, we say nothing to the boys. But we often wonder if they think that American life is run on missionary principles. The boys are taught that smoking is a sin. That is only one instance. On Sundays, they are not allowed to leave the college grounds except to go over to the Armenian Protestant Church for the afternoon service. Taking walks is taboo. What do you think of that? We easily forego the smoking. It is a question of example to boys: and we see the reasonableness of the point of view. But we simply cannot stay indoors on these glorious days.

We always take the same Sunday morning walk: for it never fails to interest us. We circle the college grounds, and climb up on a mound, under which Cleopatra's castle or Sardanapalus's tomb is supposed to be. There we hear the boys singing. They are wonderful singers, and we love to listen to the familiar hymn tunes. Last Sunday a Moslem wedding was being celebrated at the same time. Men in gay-coloured jackets and sashes were moving toward the house where the wedding was taking place: others were already around the door. A native orchestra was playing. The instruments were squeaking reed whistles, two-stringed guitars and drums. You can imagine the music they give forth, when I add that they never get off the minor key. On the flat roof a group of women, veiled and silent, huddled pathetically together. The blending of heathenish music with a Moody and Sankey hymn was indescribable.

Crossing the open space from the mound to the Mersina road, we see ill-kept cattle trying to get grass to keep them from starvation. Sometimes there is a sick or aged horse brought here to die. With all the frightful cruelty to animals everywhere evident, Orientals strangely enough will not kill animals. They do not put out of misery beasts suffering from their neglect and cruelty. This distorted kindness comes to cap the climax of misery for patient burden-bearers broken with toil. When an animal falls by the roadside, and the owner cannot whip or kick it into going farther, he just leaves it there. In riding we see frequently the remains of a camel or a horse. In spite of wanting to avoid the offense to nostrils as well as the struggle with a mount shying for good reason, we have to pass by. For the carcass is generally right alongside the road, and we cannot always make a detour through the fields. Filthy jackals skulk away at our approach, howling in savage protest and yet trembling with fear of us.

We pass out of the town to the Mersina road under an interesting arch, called St. Paul's gate. It is one of the gates of the old walled city, but whether it is of Roman, Byzantine or Arabic origin it is impossible to tell. In Tarsus and all around Tarsus there are numerous archaeological remains. But they have been so defaced and mutilated and built over that it is hard to get any idea at all of the original construction. The natives declare that the Mersina gate was built by Harun-al-Rashid, hero of the *Arabian Nights*. Harun's walls did pass at this point, and the city has never gone beyond. A few yards outside the gate, we are in a Fellahin village. Between two of the reed huts is a mud oven, patted into oval form, baked outside by the sun and inside by a fire of grass. When we pass, the women are always making bread. The whole operation is before your eyes.

The wheat is threshed out of its stalks and winnowed, and ground in a stone basin with a huge pestle of iron or copper. The coarse flour is mixed with water, and kneaded in pats about as big as my hand. These are passed to an old hag, who quickly flattens them out on a board, using her forearm as rolling-pin. They are put in the oven with sticks. Two or three minutes—and you have your bread. It is not in loaves. Think of a griddle-cake nine inches in diameter, or something even thinner than a griddle-cake, and you have the Fellahin bread. It is splendid wrapping paper. When there are no fig-leaves at hand, the peasants give you butter and cheese done up in bread.

The Cydnus River runs through and around Tarsus in a dozen branches, all of which do the quadruple service of mill races, drinking troughs for man and beast, washing places for man and beast and carriage and clothes, and irrigation ditches. There is plenty of water and it runs so fast that there is always time for it to get clean for the user below. Tarsus is full of mills: cotton, sesame, flour and saw-mills. One of the largest cotton-mills—for ginning and weaving both—is on the Mersina road. Here we stop to watch and tease the turtles in the mill-race. They are lined up on the bank, generation after generation of them—like a family group for a photograph in New England (of the old days only, alas!). The timid ones flop into the water at our approach. Most of them, however, are insolently indifferent.

Our idea is to make them all "*vamoose.*" We throw pieces of sugar-cane at them, and Herbert, everlasting kid, is not satisfied until only

44

ungraceful claws, wildly waving above the surface of the water, reveal where the sprawling creatures have taken refuge. Not a head dares appear: for Herbert is near baseball days, and sugar-cane is heavy enough to carry straight. In the wider water beyond the mill, we frequently see long shapeless ridges of brown-black shifting lazily about, moving just enough to show that they are not mud-banks. A rude cart stands on the edge of the stream and on its pole is fastened a double-yoke. Those ridges are the buffaloes that belong to the cart. The lumbering beasts sway back and forth through the streets dragging incredibly high and heavy loads of cotton-bales to the railroad.

Occasionally they are unhitched and allowed to get into the water for a rest and a bath. There they lie in the gray mud, absolutely relaxed, languidly flapping their ears to splash water on their heads. Our walk ends at the bridge half a mile beyond the cotton factory. West of the bridge the Adana-Mersina road enters the great Cilician Plain once more after the long break of Tarsus and its suburbs. Half a dozen broken places in this bridge are a constant menace to horse and camel. It keeps getting worse and worse. An enormous traffic passes over it: but does anyone think of mending it? They will wait until it falls down. The motto of this country is every man for himself. There is no public spirit—no idea of the common weal. One is moved only by what affects him directly, and acts only for what he believes is his interest. But none sees farther than *immediate interest*. Tomorrow is in God's hands. The Young Turk regime, on which we see the American newspapers and magazines publishing extravagant eulogies—how will it succeed? The governing classes in Islam cannot be regenerated until Islam is imbued with a different spirit—self-sacrifice, initiative, thought of the future.

Every day we look out of our window to see what there is to see. This is no idle curiosity or idle waste of time—there is always some sight to be memorized, visualized, and tucked away in your mind for future reference. A little group of haggard, prematurely old women, with veils over their heads, and tall green or terra-cotta water-bottles on their bent shoulders, passes by. The women of the poor wear shabby black bloomers, shoes without stockings, gay-coloured blouses open at the throat, and on their heads veils made of cheese-cloth. One corner of the veil they hold in their teeth, so that but half of their hopelessly tired, haunting, unhappy faces can be seen. Only the children and the men look happy at all. Very early the lines of care and cruelty are indelibly pencilled upon girl-faces.

Half a dozen horses bravely struggle along under the weight of an odd-looking burden: the bakeries here burn in their ovens green branches of a kind of resinous bush that grows in the foothills and mountains. The bush is gathered and bound into rough bundles, and put in bulging loads on the groaning pack-saddles of uncomplaining horses. The horse is hidden in his leafy burden. A passing train looks like a moving forest. One could believe Shakespeare had been here to get the idea of the Burnham beeches moving to Dunsinane!

Childish voices call up hopefully: "*Madama.*" I see sometimes as many as a dozen children holding out their hands. Some girls have tiny babies strapped to their backs. I go to the window armed with savoury ammunition, and before I know it these fascinating young ones have charmed away all my store of dates and figs and candies from the last day in Mersina.

If you look higher than the street you see a sky-line that leads from flat grass-topped roofs, through the town, up to the foot-hills. Domes mean mosques, when flanked by minarets. The minarets are tall, slender and pointed at the top. Where the cone begins, a door opens to a small iron-railed ledge, and here it is that the *muezzin* walks when he sings the chant that calls the faithful to prayer. You know as you look at these minarets at the hour of prayer that men are lying prostrate before each of the mosques, and more men are grouped around the city fountains washing their feet in preparation for prayer. It is not pleasant to think of the curse against "*infidels*" in the call to prayer— even if the *muezzin* has a sweet voice that rings out over the houses and comes to you mingled with the sweeter voice of the *muezzin* in a more distant minaret.

Away to the left are the beloved Taurus mountains. They are never-failing—and we look at them with new eyes every day. As we go down to breakfast, we stop just a minute to see the colour and outline of these old friends. We can distinguish the pass that leads to Namrun—and often in the moonlight we think of the lovely night last autumn when we rode into Tarsus while the deep rich bell of the clock-tower was ringing. The clock strikes the hour, then after a pause of two minutes repeats it. Splendid idea: for you can check up on your first count.

A whole letter could be written about what we see from the windows. Whatever I write, the culmination, the climax, must be the camels. They are the best of all "sights" to me. The first I saw were in Smyrna, or rather just outside of Smyrna, taking refuge under a clump of trees from the noon-day sun. It was a group of at least thirty, the most camels I had ever seen together in my life. I wanted then to stop, but we were *en route* for Polycarp's tomb, and had only a few hours ashore. Now I have camels to my heart's delight and satisfaction. But never enough! Our street is one of the roads to the market-place. During the autumn, when much wood and cotton was being transported, camels passed under my window every morning. About six o'clock they began. Train after train wound slowly along. The camels travel single file, fastened from saddle to saddle.

Until I came to Turkey, I had seen few camels outside of a zoo. The only loose one I remember is the camel ridden in Paris by the beggar that used to haunt the Place Saint-Michel. No two camels are alike. In a hundred that pass, each is different from the one ahead, very different. Camels are just as different as people. They are dark brown, tawny brown, on and on through the various shades up to the palest tan. The colours run from that one gets from polishing russet shoes with the black shoe brush to that produced by whitewashing a dust-covered wall. The shades are the echoes of the blending shifting tones of desert sand. The wide cushioned foot speaks fervently of the silence and patience of the camel's journeyings to and fro. The camel's eye is sorrowful. His air is supercilious, as if his claim to aristocracy among animals was forever settled by the fact that he was the favourite of Mohammed.

CHAPTER 6

Hamlet and the Gathering of the
Storm Clouds

April seventh, Nineteen-Nine.

Dear Mother:

There's an awful lot of knowledge,
That you never get at college.

But I tell you, my dear, I am glad that Anna Bess put me on the scenery committee the first time 1906 had a play. Ever since I left Bryn Mawr I have been looking for the things I learned that were "going to prove useful in after years." For the first time I've hit something. When the boys wanted to get up a play I showed them how to put squares of canvas together, tacked on poles at the platform end of the big schoolroom. I marked out a court scene with charcoal, and painted it in. One advantage of making scenery here is that paint dries quicker than it did in the cellar of our dormitory.

I economized time by sewing costumes while the boys rehearsed. It was the most unimaginable sort of rehearsing. For the play was to be given in Turkish, of which Jeanne and I understood not a word. All the same with my little red leather-bound English Shakespeare stuck in the corner of the divan near my lapful of sewing, I was supposed to criticize the acting. I kept looking from needle to book to actor. Jeanne, on the other side of the divan, was following in a French translation. Hamlet and Ophelia dashed around while I put ermine on the king's coat. The boys would not listen to cutting. They were game for the whole play—not quailing before scenes that Irving and Terry could not swing. They have prodigious memories. We found that out when one of them memorized Herbert's entire lecture on the Rise of the Papacy, and gave it afterwards as answer to a question in term examination. Their patience and endurance are limitless. They never get bored.

Jeanne and I were back of the scenes on the great night to start the play with everybody dressed and bewigged, painted and securely hitched together. Clothes had to be sewed on the ladies. The boys entered so fully into the spirit of the thing that when the show was actually on, they hadn't time to think about their clothes. My red Cretan rug, firmly strapped to the shoulders of Hamlet's mother, made a real court train. (The actors had practised not to walk on it. Luckily they learned this early in the rehearsals, when Ophelia, passing his future mother-in-law, stepped on the Cretan rug and "sat down too much" on the hard schoolroom floor.) Crowns and wigs had to be anchored with adhesive tape.

Ophelia, young and rather slender for his age, was capable of the martyrdom of forcing his feet into my satin dancing slippers. It was possible only when I made him wear my silk stockings. His own knitted socks were much too thick for stage purposes as well as for slippers. A schoolroom bench, assisted by the boxes of two croquet games and covered by rugs, made a passable throne. The stage manager was dismayed when he realized that Doctor Christie's pulpit was screwed fast to the platform. I discovered that the top of the pulpit could be removed, and comforted the boys by pointing out to them that those in the audience who had ever seen a real theatre would certainly think the pulpit was a prompter's box.

The audience of students and teachers was increased by the parents of boys living in Tarsus and local Moslem dignitaries, the *kaïmakam*, the *feriq* and the *mufti*. [1] They were delighted to come, and praised our school and its hospitality. At the end of each scene they applauded conspicuously. The *mufti's* parchment-like cheeks wrinkled to expose his yellow gumless teeth in an appreciative grin, while the *kaïmakam* shook hands with the asthmatic *feriq pasha* until his Hamidian decorations jingled on his breast.

Our efforts to persuade the boys to cut out a part here and there were in vain. They insisted on giving the whole blessed thing. Candied

---

1 The *Kaïmakam* is at the head of the civil administration of the municipality, the *Feriq* of the military administration, and the *Mufti* of the religious administration. Civil and military government and religion are all closely connected—essential factors in Turkish society. Constantinople has its hold directly on every community in Turkey.

almonds and glasses of water passed around in the audience helped to keep them awake. The atmosphere was hot and close, and the petroleum was getting low in the lamps. Between the first and second acts the school band—all individualists—did their favourite piece, the very march that the old German orchestra leader in Philadelphia used to play at the Country Club dances just after the last waltz before supper. The boys put the vigour of their youth and the enthusiasm of the occasion into their playing. I was glad the venerable *mufti* had cotton in his ears. The place was already so full of people and talk and lamp-baked air that I thought the floor of the dormitory above would spill down on us when the band thundered a climax of horns, trombones, drums and cymbals.

As the play went on, the audience did not need candied almonds or music to keep them awake. Things began to go badly for Hamlet's mother's husband. People stopped fanning. The dignitaries moved uneasily in their places. With heads hunched down in their shoulders, they kept their eyes glued on the stage. They are not familiar with our great William, and believe, no doubt, that we invented the play as well as the actors' costumes. Horror of horrors! We had forgotten what they might read into the most realistic scene. An Armenian warning for Abdul Hamid? The assassins mastered the struggling king. He lay there with his red hair sticking out from his crown, and the muscles of his neck stiffened as he gasped for breath while his throat was cut with a shiny white letter-opener.

As I fell asleep last night, I saw the three dignitaries leaning forward frowning. The *mufti* had clinched the sides of the bench with his thin hands. Could they be seriously disapproving of our show, because we killed a king in it? I went to sleep laughing over Doctor Christie's story of the way the authorities would not permit him to teach physics in the early days because he was obliged to use the word "revolution."

April ninth.

Last night Herbert and I drove on the Mersina road. We love this drive in the late afternoon. It leads in the direction of home—straight to the sunset. Camels came towards us. From the head the line was double. As they parted to the sides of the road, I said to Herbert, "Let's count the beasts. You take your side and I'll take this." They numbered more than two hundred, all laden with petroleum tins.

★★★★★★

We drove again this evening. Even walking is proscribed for me now. I can go out of the college grounds only in a carriage, and then not far. In a Moslem quarter, on a road between vegetable gardens, boys threw stones—the first time it has happened to us. As Charlemagne was nervous and reared from being hit several times, Herbert did not dare to get out and leave me alone. There was nothing to do but drive on, and accept the stoning. I was hit on the left shoulder—a big stone it was. The bruise is painful.

April thirteenth.

Could not finish for Thursday's post. We have had Easter to think about—examinations, and the boys going off for their ten days.

Miss Talbot has come to stand by me. Isn't she a dear? Imagine a soft-voiced English woman of the upper class being a trained nurse, and *my* nurse—when there is none in the world for me to turn to. It seems as if she has been dropped from Heaven at my door. Miss Talbot is a woman of independent means, who studied nursing to equip herself for doing good. She came out here to Turkey to find work at her own expense. She is going into mission dispensary nursing, but thinks just now that I am "the duty at hand." Lucky for me!

The annual meeting of the American Mission is being held in Adana this week. It opens tomorrow. Dr. Christie and Miner, of course, had to go, and they persuaded Herbert to go with them. It was a chance for him to meet the missionaries from the interior, and get an idea of mission problems. Herbert was very anxious to meet the missionaries of whom we have been hearing so much. They are to reach Adana overland on horse from Marash, Hadjin, Aintab and other stations. It is the jubilee year—the fiftieth annual meeting. The native Protestant pastors of this whole field are to hold a reunion at the same time. An important question is coming before the Mission—what to do with the orphanages that were established after the massacres of 1894-96. The orphans are practically all grown up now.

I urged Herbert to go. It is only forty miles, and he can return tomorrow if we have news to telegraph him. Miss Talbot thinks it is all right, and her being here reassures him. He needs only to be gone one night. At the last minute he hesitated, but I pushed him out with the others.

As we said goodbye, Herbert stood below me in the school grounds, and I was on the steps a few feet above, leaning over and talking to him. Just for fun, I took his *fez* off—a black velvet *fez*. My giggle and smile died away as I idly twirled that *fez* around my finger. Sometimes in the sunshine one sees the shadow of Islam. After all, wouldn't he be safer in a hat? I put this into words. Herbert scoffed at the idea, but he humoured me and went to find his gray felt hat.

Must go to marking examination papers of my rhetoric class. Can you imagine me an English reader like Miss Marsh? You were afraid three lectures a week and two rhetoric lessons would be a lot for me to manage, but Mother dear, these boys are hungry for an education. I long for a copy of one of the rhetorics we used at college. Have improvised a text book. Coaxed it out of my memory. I averaged two hours a day, typewriting the material on our Hammond. The boys drink in my stupid lectures the way the Cilician Plain drinks in the first autumn rains. I gave a stiff quiz just after the Easter vacation. I am continuing the daily themes and the critical papers. I have learned a lot from the boys about the fable in Turkish literature. Also about habits of camels, and the real Abraham Lincoln. Can't you see me rehashing Bryn Mawr English and adapting it to the Tarsians?

CHAPTER 7

The Storm Approaches

Wednesday, April fourteenth.

Mother:

This afternoon I sent Socrates to the station with the buggy (the word is not misused—we have a real American one). Herbert was to return by the afternoon train. An hour later, Socrates came back alone and told me that "bad things" were happening in Adana. There was a massacre starting. Yesterday four Armenian women were killed. This morning there was killing begun in vineyards just outside of the town. While he was telling me this news, a telegram mercifully arrived from Herbert. It read: "*Reviendrai demain. Aujourd'hui tout bien.*" Herbert's French is far from what it might be. But telegrams in English are not accurately transmitted in Turkey.

When I went over to Mrs. Christie's sitting-room for afternoon tea, I found several Armenian women there, among them the mothers of two of our teachers. One mother was begging for permission for her son to sleep at the college. He came later, bringing his precious violin, which he asked me to hide for him. I put it back of our bathtub. The other mother was in tears. Her son is in Adana for the holidays with his bride. This poor woman has a right to fear. She lost two children in the 1895-96 massacres. One little girl was trampled to death by a squad of Turkish soldiers. The son, our Armenian professor,—the one in Adana—was saved with the greatest difficulty, having been hidden for several days in the dark corner of a mill.

Excitement grew this afternoon. Patrols are going through the streets. We are told that this is done to calm people. The unrest is showing itself. I asked Socrates not to repeat what he had seen and heard. Panic is contagious. He was unmoved by my caution. He shook his head, saying, "It is going to be very terrible, very terrible."

53

I wish it were not Easter vacation. So many of our boys have gone to their villages. They would be safer here. Dr. Christie and Herbert and Miner would not be in Adana. If this had to occur, why not when college was going, and we were all together? The regular routine would do much to keep minds occupied. When you are busy, you are normal, no matter what may be going on around you.

Thursday, April fifteenth.

Mother dear:

I wasn't afraid last night. I slept the whole night through. This morning there was quite a crowd of Armenians in the school dining-room. They look to us for protection and food and shelter. They are terror-stricken, and have reason to be. How would you like to live in a country where you knew your government not only would not protect you, but would periodically incite your neighbours to rob and kill you *with the help of the army?*

Socrates asked to be allowed to go to the station again to see if Herbert came by the morning train. Off he trotted, leaving me to my sewing. He came back in the greatest excitement. At the station all was confusion. People jumped off the train, and shouted madly that the whole of Adana was burning. Immediately a mob formed, and some of these men seized the buggy and made off with it, leaving Socrates to get home as best he could. Henri Imer had gone over on horseback, and he had a bad time too. His horse was struck by a Turk, but he succeeded in getting away. He went right to the barracks and found the buggy there. Henri secured permission for Socrates to bring it home.

Another telegram has come from Herbert saying, "*Tout bien. Retournerai Tarsous aussitôt que possible, peut-être pas avant demain*"

The afternoon train failed to appear.

Just before dark, the boys of the sub-freshman class who were spending the Easter vacation at the college came and told me they wanted to be my bodyguard. They are to sleep tonight on my balcony—the balcony on the inside of the building just outside my bedroom. Their beds, mattresses and blankets have been given to refugee women for the little children. It is April—but still cold at night. I have taken from the walls and floors all our Turkish rugs—every single one of our treasures—and spread them on the boards for the boys to sleep on—or under. They mean absolutely nothing to me. I do not care if they are lost in the confusion.

Johnny tells me there is not much oil in my lamp. I cannot be without light. It may be needed badly in the night. It may be vital for me to have light. To get candles and petroleum from the large school-building was impossible for the boys. The precious things might be taken from them in the crowd. For our compound is filling: and many of the refugees we do not know at all. I must go with the boys. I shall take Kevork and Samsun as well as Socrates. To be without Herbert at a time like this! These blessed boys of mine are splendid. They are thoughtful, devoted, courageous, and most delicate in their attention. I could not be in better hands.

The best in people comes out at a crisis. If I live through these days, I shall never cease to cry out against the supercilious, superficial travellers, who, enjoying a sheltered life for themselves and their loved ones, say mean things about Armenians—even that they deserve to be massacred—that massacres are their own fault. All I can say is this: May God Almighty forgive them their judgments, for they know not what they say. My Armenian boys and my Greek Socrates are every bit as fine, every bit as thoroughbred, as Anglo-Saxon boys of the best blood and training.

I am back safely—with oil and candles, too. Now I am ready for what may come in the night.

In the assembly-room of the big school-building, some of the refugees had gathered around the pastor of the Protestant Church. It was an impromptu prayer-meeting. They were singing hymns. I do not understand Turkish, but, as they use our tunes, I knew the hymns. It was a comfort to steal in, and sit down for a while among my fellow-sufferers. Only eight months ago, when we first came to Cilicia, and went to church up in the Taurus Mountains summer place, I remember how queer these people looked to me. They belonged to another world. I was an outsider. I had difficulty in understanding some traits of their character. I was hasty in my judgment of them—hasty through ignorance. I was impatient with their constant fear of what "might happen any time" to Christians living under Moslem rule.

I had no conception of what "might happen any time"—that was why. During the singing, I looked up to the ceiling. The trapdoor brought back vividly the day when Daddy Christie had showed it to me, saying, "We have that for use in time of massacre." I had laughed. The constitutional era was here. Those were things of the past. Probably it is a mercy that youth and inexperience make one refuse to believe that bad things—horrible things—which have happened to others may come in one's own life.

We sang softly (for the sound must not get outside) "Lead, Kindly Light." The hymn had never meant so much to me. For, until now, there never had been "encircling gloom." I understand now. Because I need the Light, I ask for it.

CHAPTER 8

The Storm Breaks

Tarsus,
Friday, April sixteenth,
Nineteen-Nine.

Mother dear:

Men came here to tell Mrs. Christie trouble was coming. Offered to send a guard for our gate. They knew that Dr. Christie and Miner Rogers and Herbert—three of the four men of the mission family—had gone away to Adana. The fellows were Kurds. They looked like brigands. Mrs. Christie put them off, saying we were not afraid. This with a calm little air as if she didn't quite realize. When I asked her about it, she replied: "Didn't you see? They wanted to get hold of the college gate." What a woman she is! Today with Armenians coming to us in greater numbers every hour, I say to myself: What if the Kurds had possession of our broad gate? From our study window I can see the Cilician Plain stretching on and on to the Taurus. The Plain today looks like a monstrous Turkish rug. It is a riot of colour, quantities of poppies and irises and other spring flowers. *Did you ever think of this: red predominates in Turkish rugs?*

Last night we learned that the train going through towards Adana had turned back at Yenidje. By this time one hundred refugees had come to us. Massacre seemed imminent. Socrates barricaded all my shutters, and watched outside my door.

This morning another telegram came from Herbert saying that he was detained, and would get back when he could. There were no trains in either direction, so we knew the whole country was upset. Rumours began to leak through about the terrible times in Adana and I knew why Herbert had not returned. This morning there were more than five hundred refugees with us.

In the course of the morning we heard that Armenians had been killed at the Tarsus station and that the station master and other employees had fled. Then there was the whistle of a train from Adana. It brought a wild mob of *bashi-bazouks*. For concentrated hatred, a *bashi-bazouk* is a smallpox germ. I saw the train vomiting forth its filthy burden. The men wore no uniforms. They were dressed in dirty white bloomer-things, with bits of carpet fastened up their legs with crisscross ropes, in place of shoes. They looked like worn out rag dolls. I saw them gather in a mud coloured fan-shaped crowd at the flimsy entrance to the Konak, where the authorities could not be quick enough in passing out guns and ammunition and other instalments of the Devil to everyone.

Then Hell broke loose. The townspeople joined themselves to this mob. Along the road that crosses the space between us and the railway they went in groups of fifty, going at an easy run and brandishing their arms, uttering low weird howls that grew in a *crescendo* of rage. They made for the Armenian quarter, the last houses of which are only one hundred and fifty yards from us.

Shooting started and continued all day. Along with the sound of the shots we could hear the screams of the dying.

All day there has been a procession of refugees. They seem to have gathered in little groups first, for they came in a few hundred at a time in pulsation. In the afternoon they came steadily. Mother! the sound of the feet of the multitude. Some poor things were wounded, some were looking for husbands or children that could not be found. They brought nothing with them. Sick women were carried on the backs of their husbands. Little children struggled to keep up with panic-stricken elders. Children, feeble old people, chronic invalids, the desperately ill, were possessed with supernatural strength.

When they reached the goal, our gate, they were like the Durando we described in the Marathon race last summer. A big fellow in the meagre guard at our gate was a host in himself. He had a hearty voice, and kept waving his arms and shouting, "Come in, everybody. Inside this gate is safety for you all! Courage, little children." Occasionally he would pick up a crying baby or a sick woman, and help them inside. It was the one cheerful kindly sight of the day—to see that soldier.

About noon from Jeanne and Henri's study I saw an attack on a house very near us. There was a low hum in the distance: then a roar, and on the second-storey balcony twenty-five *bashi-bazouks* climbed, bursting in the door to the house of the richest man in Tarsus. There was shooting and screaming: then flying bits of burning paper came out of the windows, followed by blue and red flames. By opening our shutters cautiously we could hear the cruel hiss of the flames and smell kerosene in the smoke. Then the rending and crashing of the floors made a deafening noise, and the sparks began to alight on our property.

This is the regular order of things,—kill, loot, burn. The Armenian quarter is the most substantial part of the city. Most of the people store cotton on the ground floor, and this, together with liberal applications of kerosene, served to make a holocaust. Now at evening time we realize our own imminent danger.

I have made tea about twenty times during the day. What a blessing you sent those provisions. Good thing we chose from among our wedding gifts the chafing-dish and the tea basket to bring along on our journey. I have given away everything I could spare. Things to drink out of are a vital necessity. I gave away my tooth-mug to a thirsty old woman, and reserved as my drinking cup the little china affair one keeps toothbrushes in on a washstand. It stands unabashed beside the smart little silver tea-kettle and spirit lamp. How I miss my oranges. Mother Christie found a stray one this morning and sent it in to me. The boys brought some charcoal and made a fire in a *mangal* in my fireplace. I have tried my hand at a *pilaf*. Kevork brought some sheep-tail grease in a bit of paper and I held my nose while I melted it and poured it into the *pilaf*. I do not see why these people do not cook with wagon grease and be done with it.

Your tins of condensed milk I have given to Mary Rogers for her baby. A mother brought her two-year-old boy to me. The poor little thing had had nothing to eat since yesterday. The whole Armenian question sums itself up for me in those big brown eyes and their kindling with sudden light as I held a bowl of warm milk to that baby's trembling mouth. I couldn't make him smile, though, for all my coaxing.

The meals of our immediate family are served in my bedroom. Mrs. Christie's house, the big dining-room, the school buildings are overflowing with refugees. It is only the most strenuous efforts of the college boys that prevent them from over-running us too. I have just my bedroom, Mary the other bedroom for herself and the baby, and Miss Talbot is in our study. Jeanne's extra bedroom eighteen women have managed to get into. Henri's study is crowded too. I am working on baby clothes to keep my mind occupied. I am making flannel nighties: there are hundreds of babies out under our trees and on the hard asphalt of the tennis court without one change of clothing.

Dear, dear, here is a woman who has been in terrible suffering all day long. Her husband and brother were with her and several times tried to flee with her. They picked her up a bit ago and started with her through the red and black streets. Overpowered, she stopped in ——'s garden and had her baby. Wrapping the baby in something and putting it in the mother's arms, the men picked her up and made the final dash for safety. We have pulled the buggy out of the carriage-house and made a place for her in the corner. She is resting nicely now.

★★★★★★

Socrates came to me and said that friends of his, Greeks like himself, have invited him to join them in an attempt to escape to Mersina. They have a dead Greek's passport for him. He asked my advice. I told him I could not take the responsibility. Danger? There is little choice—staying here or trying to get away. I told him to go off by himself to think it over. He came back to tell me this: "You are alone. If you have to run away, you have nobody to go with you. Professor Gibbons—no one knows where he is. I will stay with you."[1]

Have been sitting on the steps leading up to the rooms of the Imers, looking out over the pathetic throng in the garden. Kevork in his snug little coat and long gingham student-apron has been sitting beside me. "You are hungry," said he. "Your future may be five minutes long. Your husband is missing. Maybe he is dead. Those telegrams were dated yesterday, you know. Your baby is not born. You cannot defend yourself or run away. *You are just like an Armenian woman.* Tell me what you think about revenge?"

Dostumian hunted wildly and fruitlessly for his mother and little

1. As a result of his heroism, Socrates (that is not his real name, but never mind) has been our ward ever since. With what aid we could give ourselves, and the help of friends to whom we have told this story, Socrates finished his college course at Tarsus, took a year in medicine at Beirut, and has since been studying at the Turkish Medical School in Constantinople. Despite the difficulty of communications between Paris and Constantinople, we have been able to follow him and help him without interruption during the years of the war in Europe. Socrates will have his medical degree in the spring of 1917. He is a loyal Turkish subject, and has done splendid work in ministering to the wounded in the Balkan War and in the present war. When the Bulgarians were attacking the defences of Constantinople, we loaned him to Major Doughty-Wylie, who was at that time in charge of the British field ambulance work. Major Doughty-Wylie recommended him for the British Red Cross medal.

sister among the crowd. Harutun urged that he, on account of his red hair, would not be taken for an Armenian. He could find them. When he got to the house, he put the mother on his back and ran to us before the *bashi-bazouks* knew what he was up to. When he took the mother, he hid the little girl in a corner by piling sticks of wood on her. Told her to keep quiet, and wait for him to come back.

By the time he returned to excavate the youngster, and had put her on his back, and climbed to the roof of the house, the *bashi-bazouks* were after him. Oh, the flat Oriental roofs! Harutun skipped from one to the other, taking amazing distances, with the child on his back. Danger is a prod. He got to a place on some roof beside which a foreign construction company had set up a pole in anticipation of the electric lighting system. Down that pole slipped Harutun. He ran like mad, and restored the youngster to her mother and her brother.

But electric lighting companies do not sandpaper their poles. Harutun's hands were cruelly torn. His first thought when he began to think of himself again was to come to me to get his hands dressed. He sat down on Herbert's steamer trunk and I picked out the splinters. I washed the wounds and bound them up with gauze and camphenol, also the palms of the hands and the wrists. He begged me to leave the fingers out so he could work. The boy was as happy as a bird: for it flooded into his brain what he had done. While his hands were still trembling from the pain and excitement, he said, "Meeses Geebons, I am not afraid to die. Dying is as natural as borning. But before I die I want to kill a Turk—just one Turk!" If his hands had not been so wrapped up in bandages, I could have shaken his right one.

After I fixed up Harutun's hands I was kept quite busy for a space with that sort of thing. A woman came and asked for some clothes for her baby and showed us the only dress she had for him. It was covered with blood—the blood of his murdered father. One dear little fellow, a favourite of Herbert's, came to me with a gash in his head. His father has been burned to death in their house and his little sister is wounded also. I prepared the bandages for a man with a gunshot wound in his neck. He was lying just outside my door. Herbert used to joke me about my emergency outfit, saying that there were enough bandages in it to do for an army, and asking how I ever expected to use sterilized catgut. Every bit of that outfit is useful now. It has saved lives!

Friday night.

Sky red with fire. Half the horizon is in flames, the whole Armenian quarter is burning. Our native teachers and boys under the direction of Henri Imer are fighting the flames valiantly. The sparks are flying toward us, driven by a heavy wind, and eternal vigilance is required to note every spark the moment it falls, to quench it in time. The blaze is so brilliant that we can read by it. A telegram came from Herbert about eleven o'clock. I signed the receipt by the light of the flames. I cannot read it. It is a mixture of Turkish and French. What I can make out is the hour of sending—this means that twenty-one hours ago he was still alive.

Our condition is becoming desperate. The fire threatens us. The fury of the mob may lead them to attack us. We are sheltering more than four thousand refugees, a wailing, terror-stricken mass, all trying to get out of bullet range.

We have not been able to get any word to the outside world: we realize now that Adana is cut off and we feel sure that our husbands are in as desperate a plight as are we. Word must go to Mersina. We have a Turkish hand-writing teacher, a Moslem, who is faithful to us. We have sent him tonight by horse with Harutun, the senior whose courage was thoroughly tested this afternoon. They rode into the jaws of death perhaps, but there is nothing else to do. Not only our lives but those of the refugees are at stake.

Nearly midnight.

We have prepared a few things in case we have to leave the place suddenly. Run? Where? Somebody or other remarked grimly enough: "Fix only what you can carry by yourself."

I came into the bedroom, and here I sit on Herbert's steamer chair. The wood fire has gone out. The room is chilly and looks so very large. One candle gives such a little light. The big blue rugs have been carried off for bedding. How bare the place seems. Oh, how lonely! The chafing-dish stands there unwashed and tilted crooked in its stand. I have torn the bed to pieces to get a blanket for my bundle. The baby basket all dainty and waiting is on the steamer trunk beside our bed. Will it cradle my little one? If it is born out in the open, at least it won't be cold, for I have taken from the basket the knitted blanket you sent me and the package of fragrant clothing inside the tiny sheet.

For some time I have had clothes ready there for after the first bath. I tied up the bundle with our double blanket, but it was too heavy for me. I have rearranged it with a small blanket, tied corner-wise. In it are diapers, a piece of tape sterilized and a pair of surgical scissors wrapped in gauze, a length of uncut flannel, and that is all. This will be heavy enough: for I must save Herbert's thesis, and that in its filing case is a pretty solid weight. Precious thesis—it won him his fellowship, and if there is any future, that thesis must go to Paris. Poor little Mariam out there in the carriage house—how I pitied her this evening. Was it only a few hours ago they brought her in? I envy her now. Her baby is born.

My reason tells me that this bundle beside me is necessary: but it seems futile. Everything has gone. One support after another has been removed. Humanly speaking, the fact of safety is gone. Am I cold-blooded, that the sense of it remains? Sufficiency of food? Gone. Human ties? Gone. No sister, no brothers, no mother, no husband. Railway communications? Gone. There is no consul at Mersina. No protection from my own government. Did you ever wonder which end of your life you are living? Kevork was right a bit ago about the future looking five minutes long. My religion has suddenly become like a solid rock, and I have planted my back right against it. Religion is simple, and it works.

Tell Herbert I have not cried once, that I am not afraid. Tell him possessions mean nothing. What good can things do? There are hundreds of gold *liras* in the safe. What good are they? I see where life stretches beyond the place money can signify.

All this time I have boosted myself up by saying, "Don't break down yet, wait for something worse." If you wait for real trouble—then you are so busy, you have no time to worry. My religion has in one night become vitally subjective. I know—because when I reason about it, I marvel at my own calm. Shall it be with me as it was with Elsie Hodge, the Bryn Mawr girl who was killed in the Boxer uprising? All day I have been thinking about her. I am writing this and shall leave it here—in case. I cannot write the words needed to describe the fate of women in my condition at the hands of these fiends. Maybe someday I can tell you.

★★★★★★

Sitting on the floor in Mary Roger's room, writing with my paper on my knee. When I left our room, I went to Herbert's wardrobe and put his overcoat on. In one pocket I stuffed Educator crackers out of the box you sent. Some fell on the floor and I left them there. A wee knitted hug-me-tight went into another, and into a third pocket I put the silk American flag Clement gave me when I was married. Miss Talbot is lying down on a cot in our study. Being a Britisher, she is able to sleep. Before I left her in the study, I got out the filing case containing Herbert's thesis. I put it down by the door here in Mary's room, right close to my feet. Then I lay down on the floor with my bundle as a pillow.

★★★★★★

We, from our darkened room where that blessed baby Rogers is sleeping quietly, have been looking out of the window. Two or three Turks pushed a pump affair up in front of a house nearby. "Humanity is not dead yet!" I thought, "they are going to try to limit the fire." The water streamed from the hose and it was kerosene. They soaked the roof. Little fingers of flame began waving in the wind. Heavy black smoke is hanging over the town. We can feel the hot air and smell the oil—like a gigantic smoking lamp. Sparks fell on the windowsill just now as I stood there. I patted them with my hands and put them out, but not before they burned little holes in the wood.

We closed the blinds and sat down cross-legged on the floor and talked quietly. About being widows. The boys must soon come back to us—either that, or they are dead. We wondered which one of us was a widow. Perhaps both.

Once Mary asked me: "Brownie, what are you praying for?"

"Goodness, Mary, I don't know what I am praying for. Guess I have just got to live with my soul opened toward Heaven."

A little later Mary spoke again, this time cheerfully, for she had thought of something: "I know, let's pray for the wind to change."

Sure enough, it was blowing in our direction. We went to the window again, never thinking of danger. *You cannot consistently keep your mind on danger to yourself.* As we looked, the flames were lying low, blue tipped with yellow, and reaching towards us. We concentrated on a change of the wind, and there was a change. The flames instead of lying low were vertical, licking and swaying. Then they lay low again, this time back on the ruined buildings. This may have been coincidence. You may think so if you like. But I believe I saw the hand of the Lord come down and forbid those flames to move farther. Never again will I have to be reasoned with to believe in miracles.

CHAPTER 9

Life and Death

Tarsus,

Saturday,

April seventeenth.

Sometime in the morning.

Mother dear:

Once that wind changed, we slept. Mary and I slept from one to three. Baby Rogers is a good little chap. Yes, my dear, *"I laid me down and slept. I awaked, for the Lord sustained me."* This is the way to learn a text—live it.

When we got awake, it was daylight. Shouting again at the gate. I ran to my study window that looks down into the street outside of the gate. Excited men were pushing and struggling. Their cries were shrill. My heart sank. Was the killing to be renewed under our eyes? Then Mary said, "They are selling bread, and want six *metallics* a loaf." The business of life goes on in spite of cataclysms. Selling bread! In the midst of life we are in death. Yes, but in the midst of death we are in life. The family goes home to dinner after the funeral. When you are living the cataclysm, however, your vision is not adjusted to the small events. The matter-of-fact things are happening because they always happen and must happen.

★★★★★★

A door outside slammed. Then the door into Mary's room opened. In came Mother Christie, looking as though she hadn't slept. The steel-rimmed spectacles used indifferently by herself and Daddy Christie, were pushed away up on her forehead. She said briskly: "Another baby! a dear little boy, and not a rag to put on him!" I went to my steamer trunk to fetch three little flannel petticoats and two *kimonos*. Down jumped the spectacles without her putting her hand on them. "No, no, my child, I cannot take them." Before I had pressed them into her arms, she had finished her protesting. Away she went, murmuring: "Give and spend and the Lord will send. That's what you think." Well, there may be time for me to make more petticoats.

They say that eight hundred houses have been burned. Many people were still in the houses. If they showed themselves, or tried to get out by windows or roofs, they were shot. It was death either way. We fear that few Armenians are alive in Tarsus outside of our compound and in the Catholic Mission nearby. The whole Armenian quarter, right up to my windows, is burning. The bright blaze persists in many places where there is yet much to feed upon.

Saturday afternoon.

We did not think of breakfast. Mary had fallen asleep again after nursing the baby. I munched biscuits in my bedroom, and then I undid on the bed the bundle I had made up in the night. The piece of flannel might be needed sooner than I could use it. So I stretched it out on the mattress, and cut four flannel petticoats. With the blinds barricaded, my only light was what filtered through the slits in the shutter of the side window. I had to keep doing something, and I did not want to go out to talk to anyone. So I found my thread and thimble, and began to make up the petticoats.

It may have been minutes or hours. I shall never know, for I had not looked at the clock when I woke. Suddenly I heard cries outside, that were taken up by the thousands in the college yard. In the mingling of voices I caught my husband's name. "Steady now," I thought. "Is this life or death?" Then Jeanne's golden head appeared at my door.

"Herbert's here," said Jeanne.

I hurried out into the study, and ran to the window with Mary and Jeanne. Daddy Christie and Herbert were at the gate, surrounded by regular soldiers. But we did not see the tall figure of Miner Rogers. Joy and apprehension were strangely mingled. I ran first to the door leading to the balcony. Up the steps came Daddy Christie. Herbert and Henri were behind, evidently trying to keep people from following them. Daddy Christie said, "Thank God, you're safe: where is Mary?" I led him to our study. People seemed to rise up from nowhere, crowding about us. Jeanne had instinctively taken Mary into her own room, and Daddy Christie followed.

It may have been minutes or hours. I shall not know. After the lapse of a few hours, it seems to me that I am writing fiction. Perhaps

66

I make it up as I go along. Never again shall I believe in the accuracy of testimony given on the witness-stand about what happened in moments of stress.

Turning so that I looked towards the double-doors, I saw Herbert standing there. Surging thoughts went through me. One was that I must not let these emotions reach the baby. I clinched will and muscles to safeguard the little thing. The other thought was to get over beside Herbert. As I made my way through the crowd toward the door, I thought: have I died and Herbert too? What was that I suffered last night? How can I know? Then the brain in my head told me: touch him, and if he is warm, it is not death. I took his left hand in my right and with my other hand touched his face. It was warm.

"Where is Miner Rogers?"

"He is dead," came the answer. Herbert's free hand reached back of him for the, doorknob. He went slowly out on the balcony, closing the door behind him, as if he did not know what he was doing.

Herbert has no recollection of this meeting. We figure out that it is because he had already been reassured about me, for he distinctly remembers seeing me at the study window as he came through the street below. The second his anxiety was relieved about me, his mind concentrated on the terrible news he and Dr. Christie were bringing to Mary.

I turned back toward the room to realize that Dr. Christie was telling Mary. This was too much for me and I went into our bedroom beyond. One sees on the stage, and reads in novels, meetings like this. Ours was not dramatic. It was natural and human. Herbert was entering the bedroom from the other door at the same moment, and when he saw me he asked: "Can you make some tea? I am hungry."

I investigated my washstand to see what I could find in the way of food. Two Turkish officers had followed Herbert into the bedroom. They were hungry, too. I took the lid off the chafing-dish. Inside were bits of bacon. The officers must have wondered why I laughed— Herbert, too. Pent-up feelings were expressed in that laugh. I realized that I had presence of mind enough not to give bacon to Moslems. The pig is an unclean beast to non-Christians. Typewriters have been smuggled into Turkey with perfect ease when packed in the middle of a box of hams.

One officer was the *Mutesarif* of Namrun, where we spent a honeymoon month last summer. He came, I suppose, to assure us of his friendliness. You ought to see how he drank tea. Just like a Russian!

And he stopped eating Uneeda biscuits only when the tin was empty. The other officer was an Albanian who spoke French. Herbert had picked him out in Adana to bring the bodyguard of soldiers that he had compelled the *vali* to give him. Herbert says we can trust him. He is under Herbert's orders, with the soldiers, as long as we need him. Herbert had no time to give me details of these days. He went out with the officers as soon as he had eaten, after telling me to stay in my rooms. Miss Talbot came in. Then Jeanne and Mary. I could give them no word of what had happened in Adana. They told me about Miner.

★★★★★★

Herbert came back soon with Daddy Christie. They had been arranging about posting the soldiers of Herbert's guard. But they said that the massacre was over, and no attack against us was to be anticipated. What they had feared was the fire. If that had driven us out in the mob—But why talk of what might have happened? What did happen was terrible enough. Miner gone, and with him Mr. Maurer, a Hadjin missionary, shot dead. Herbert and Lawson Chambers, a Y. M. C. A. travelling secretary, were down in the town when the massacre started. They did not get back to the Armenian quarter at all. They telegraphed Major Doughty-Wylie. He and Mrs. Doughty-Wylie took the last train that went through to Adana. The major was shot in the street. His arm held up in front of him saved him. Herbert says he left him this morning in bed, and with a fever. Daddy Christie told us what had happened at the Mission and in the Armenian quarter. Then Herbert began his story. He had just started when there was a knock at the door. Someone wanted Dr. Christie. He went out. In a moment he came back and called Herbert. We waited. That is woman's sphere—waiting.

Young Miner cried in the next room. Mary went to him. What a blessing she had that baby! I told Jeanne she had better go and stand by her. Herbert returned—alone. He had a bit of paper in his hand. He gave it to me, saying that it had just been brought through from Mersina. It read:

> No ships yet—massacre expected any minute. Cannot rely on authorities.

It had been brought by an Armenian who reported the country full of Kurds. We seemed safe for the moment in Tarsus. Herbert put it right up to me. The Albanian officer and the soldiers were under

68

his command. The train he had seized in Adana was still at the station. He could try to get down the line to Mersina. His coming—with the soldiers—might stave off the massacre for a few hours. The ships were bound to reach Mersina soon.

I had no choice, Mother. It all seemed so simple—the only thing to do. It is still life or death, and we don't know which. But we do know each step as we go along. I put my hands on Herbert's shoulders to hold myself up. For I only pretend to strength and courage. I really have neither. And I said to him: "You are all the world to me, but I must remember that you are only one man to the world."

He answered: "Of course. That's the way it is. I shall try my best to get back tonight." He kissed me and went out. We would both have lost our nerve if we had talked longer. I'm glad he hurried. I threw myself on the bed and cried. Then I remembered Mary, and was ashamed of myself.

Just for something to do I have tried to go back over the day and put it down for you. People have come in. When they saw I was writing they went away. Now Mother Christie arrives to tell me that I simply must come and eat. They have managed to get a real meal together—the first in two days. It is way after six o'clock.

April eighteenth.

Herbert did not go to Mersina. He came back last night—or rather I brought him back. At supper—a meal of sorrow—Daddy Christie received a telegram. The lines are working. That has been a mystery these past few days. They stopped the railway, but why didn't they cut the telegraph? And, in the midst of killing and looting and burning, we have received telegrams delivered coolly by an *employé* who stepped over the dead to get to us. The telegram was from Adana, stating that the British cruiser *Swiftsure* had arrived at Mersina.

I felt like a condemned man reprieved at the gallows. But had Herbert started? A little while before he had sent a soldier up from the station with a message saying that he found his locomotive gone, and had been trying to get another out from Mersina by using the railway's private wire. He might still be there. He need not undertake the trip now. Broken viaducts in the dark—rails torn up—Kurds wildly prancing around and shooting from their horses.

I said nothing to the others at the table. I slipped quietly out of the room, hurried up to our apartment, put on my riding-boots and Herbert's raincoat (I am glad I am pretty tall—only the sleeves needed a tuck), and made my way to the gate. I had the barn lantern we use in the stable. I did not want to risk Socrates or any of the Armenian boys. They were still killing stray ones—especially at night. The four soldiers left remonstrated. They could not understand me any more than I could understand them. They tried to bar the way. But they did not dare touch me. So they decided to resign themselves to the inevitable. Two of them came along with me.

It was a weird mile with only the lantern to light us. One soldier went in front, finding the path, and the other was beside me. From occasional zigzags I suspected what we were avoiding. Mercifully I could not see. Finally we reached the station. Herbert and his officer and the telegraph operator were in the little ticket office. Herbert was at the end of his patience—he just couldn't get up a locomotive. When he heard my news, he was very happy. The Albanian officer was not. He was for the adventure. Doubted if the news was true. Why hadn't the Mersina operator mentioned it? Just then a message went through for Adana about a special train for the British Government. The operator told us. We knew then that it was true.

Back we went, all of us. I did not ask Herbert any more about his interrupted story of the days in Adana. I did not want to hear. He did not want to tell. We found a funny story that had been sent to us for Christmas, and of which we had read only a few chapters. We reread those—and the rest of the book, laughing ourselves to sleep to save our sanity.

CHAPTER 10

Why?

Tarsus, April twenty-second.

Dearest Mother:

I have been sewing and helping care for the wounded.

Mrs. Christie gave me the first relief money that came, a Turkish gold-piece, worth four dollars and forty cents. With it I bought a roll of flannel. On Jeanne's balcony I fixed a hand-run sewing machine. There I basked in the sunshine as I worked on baby nightgowns all day Sunday. When I tell you that I made twelve nighties in a day you know the machine did speed-work. Our caldrons are all in use heating water so that mothers can wash their children and their children's clothes, and take advantage of the sunshine to dry things. Every time I finish a nightie, it means another baby can have a bath. We have contrived sanitary arrangements, and small trenches have been dug for drainage. Queer the Turks never thought of turning off our water. It could have been done easily through the surface pipes.

Dr. Peeples of the Covenanter Mission was the first doctor to come through. He got here before his supplies. I shall never forget his face when I showed him my table with the Red Cross kit. He appropriated the medicine-case and some bandages and marched off with them. Dr. Peeples and I dressed wounds. But Mother Christie stopped that on account of "my condition." Afterwards we compromised. I installed a table inside my door and worked away preparing medicines and dressings. I handed these out to the doctor on a tray, curving my wrist around the door-jamb and so was spared the pain of seeing the patients. I do not take stock in the popular notion that I might "mark the child." Only the pleasant things that happen to me can touch that child.

The arrival of the British battleship *Swiftsure* has saved Mersina.

Yesterday the commander went to Adana by special train. On his return he stopped at Tarsus and invited Dr. Christie and Herbert to accompany him to Mersina. They accepted with alacrity.

Early this morning Herbert boarded the *Swiftsure* and had a chat with the captain. As a result, the captain allowed six officers to come to Tarsus with Herbert by special train today. We had them for lunch and took them all over the city, showing them the work of the mob. When the refugee children saw these officers arrive, the poor kiddies were terrified. Many ran and hid, and the wee ones found their mothers as quickly as possible. The officers' uniforms were the cause, according to the kiddies' own words. How is that for proof that Turkish soldiery helped in the massacring!

We believe that one hundred were killed in Tarsus and four hundred in villages nearby. Adana's murders are in the thousands. The killing of Miner brings the tragedy right into our mission family. Mary is supernaturally calm and brave. Not only does she do everything for her baby, but she is in the midst of all the relief work.

While Herbert was in Mersina, Mrs. Dodds of the Covenanter Mission urged him to take me there so as to get me away from the danger of contracting some disease. She also urged that the discomfort of our now crowded quarters at Tarsus was not good for me. We have nearly five thousand refugees on the college grounds. If railroad communication is re-established before my baby comes, we are going to accept the invitation of Mrs. Dodds. I do not know from day to day and cannot plan.

Mother, if I am not ready for the sceptics, and for those who smile and jeer, yes, jeer is the word, at missionaries! The stick-in-the-muds who thought we came all this long way because we wanted adventure must be wagging their narrow little heads and wagering that we are getting more than we bargained for. I am a great believer in letting everyone have his point of view. But generally one finds that the people who boast that they are liberal and broadminded are the most bigoted people on earth. They assert their point of view, but are unwilling to admit another's right to his. One does not have to believe in missions or want to be a missionary. But one does not have to ridicule missionary effort and missionaries, either.

Among the missionaries here, women as well as men, not a single one has shown the white feather. Quite the contrary, I doubt if any other score of Americans in the United States would have upheld better the glorious traditions of our race for coolness, resourcefulness, and ability to grapple suddenly with a crisis. The American women here are made of the same stuff as my several times great-grandmother in Lebanon Valley, who carried the gun around the room together with the broom as she did her sweeping.

I can never think of the Armenians without a stirring of the heart in affection and admiration. How can Americans resist the call to help people who have the courage to die for their faith? One has to be brought to their level of suffering, to be put into the situation in which they have lived during centuries of Turkish oppression, to understand them. Mother, they are heroes—these Armenians, children and grandchildren of heroes. It is nothing spectacular that they have done, except in periods of massacre like this. But all along *they have kept the faith*, they have preserved their distinct nationality, when an easy path lay before them, were they willing to turn from Christ to Mohammed. I see now so vividly what they have been born to, what they grow up from early childhood fearing. Is not the greatest heroism in the world the silent endurance of oppression that cannot be remedied, the bending of the neck to the yoke when there is no other way, the living along normally under the shadow of a constant and justified fear of death and worse?

What saved the Tarsians the other night? Any dread of international complications? Any respect for our government? What do the Kurds know about us? Nothing. Last summer when we were camping far up in the Taurus mountains above the timber-line, a fellow of the type who has been doing the dirty work for the party in power at Stambul, came along to talk with us. We had chopped down a scrub pine-tree to build a fire and were sitting around the fire after supper. We were eating walnuts. I offered him some. With them I gave salt. He took both walnuts and salt, touched them to his forehead by way of thanks, and began to eat. Socrates expressed satisfaction that the man had done this—said we could be surer now that he would not turn fierce dogs loose the next day, when we broke camp. In talking to the man, I asked him what he knew about my country. He was a shepherd, and had never seen a town bigger than Tarsus. He replied, "There are a great many Americans in America, at least five thousand, all very rich and all very kind."

What saved the Tarsians? St. Paul's College. Those people have had the vision held up before them, and some of its light must have got into their dark hearts. I keep thinking of the way Jesus forgave people because they just didn't know what they were doing. I do not believe for a minute that it was the American flag that saved the Christian population of this town. The Stars and Stripes mean nothing to them. It is the way Daddy and Mother Christie have lived before these Turks all these years that did it.

Listen to this, and you will see what I mean. Three hundred refugees owe their lives directly to one act of thoughtful kindness. Sometime before the massacre, Dr. Christie heard that the only son of a village *sheik* had died. He got on his horse and went straight out to comfort the old father. The news came late in the day, so that Daddy Christie was obliged to make the trip in the night. I have seen the *sheik* several times myself. He came one day and invited Herbert and me to go hunting with him. He is a superb specimen. In the midst of the heat and hatred of last Friday, the *sheik* appeared with some three hundred Armenians. The order to massacre had come, "and a massacre is good hunting, you know," he blandly remarked. "As I was about to go forth, I reflected that the people here were Dr. Christie's friends. Cannot see why you like them," he added, "but seeing you do, here they are." The old man, of course, is a Moslem. He told us he found some of those he brought in hiding in the swamps, not far from his home, "lying in the water, with just their noses sticking out to breathe," he laughingly explained.

CHAPTER 11

Abdul Hamid's Last Day

Mersina,
April twenty-fifth.

Mother dear:

I wish you knew right now that we are at the Dodds in Mersina. It would relieve your mind of anxiety that must be weighing on you. But we cannot send an optimistic, reassuring cablegram. In the first place it would not be true. Then no message must go out whose chance publication in the newspapers would tend to make the world believe that danger here is passed. The powers might relax what diplomatic pressure they are exercising at Constantinople—might even recall warships or stop others that we hear are coming. Herbert is getting out the news by smuggling to Cyprus. He feels the responsibility of every word that is telegraphed. So we send you no message at all. There is still fear of a second and a worse outbreak. The massacre is not over yet.

Early yesterday morning we learned that a train would go down the line to Mersina at the usual hour. I packed what baby things I had left, and a steamer trunk with a few of our clothes. Miss Talbot said she was ready. My Armenian physician saw that the chance was excellent to get to the coast in our company. He had a valid reason for accompanying me. We took his whole family under our wing. His brother, a boy just turning into the twenties, has lost his mind—we hope only temporarily—as a result of the strain we have been under. The boy got it in his head that I alone could save him. He has been camping outside our door, and fumbling with our shutters at night. My subfreshmen kept an eye on him, but I have had to humour him. As he is my physician's brother, and there has been no way of secluding him, I have had to do this. The boy insisted on sitting in my compartment on

75

the journey yesterday. He kept me in sight. Once arrived in Mersina, they were able to take him away to a friend's house.

We reached Mersina in time for lunch, where Mrs. Dodds—the soul of kindness and solicitude—had kept rooms for us in her apartment. Mrs. Dodds' little daughter, Mary, is a wonderful child—just like her mother in wanting to be constantly doing things for other people. The atmosphere of this home is so sweet and wholesome that it makes me proud of my Covenanter ancestry and wonder if certain religious beliefs I have always thought were narrow and absurd have not their place and their reason. I asked Herbert about Covenanters last night, and found that he knew less than I did. For a parson just out of Princeton Seminary, my husband is astonishingly ignorant of theology. He doesn't seem to know or care anymore about doctrines than I do. Until last night, we had never talked about theology, and then the conversation languished after a few sentences.

Just after lunch two Turkish transports appeared off Mersina. They came inside the line of warships, and began to disembark troops in the barges that went out immediately to greet them. From the windows of the Dodds' living-room we could see the barges returning laden with soldiers. My eyes would not shut tight enough to dim the flash of the sunshine on the waves and on the blood-red *fezzes*. Herbert declared that he must go down to the *scala* to see them land. I did not want to prevent him, for I felt just as he did. Why couldn't I go too? It didn't seem to be "just the thing for one in my condition," but you know, Mother, that I can't live without exercise, and I have been impressing now for nearly a year upon Herbert two things: that I need out-of-doors as much as a fish needs water; and that I can go anywhere and do anything he does. I shall never let him get the idea into his head that I am barred from phases of his life just because I am a woman! Not a bit of it! Herbert had to take his wife along.

A disreputable looking lot they were, wretchedly clad and shod, and topped off with mussy, faded *fezzes*. We were told that they had come from Beirut to restore order in Cilicia. They had taken part in the Macedonian movement last summer, and were regiments whose officers adhered to the "Young Turk" movement, and could be relied upon to check any attempt to renew the massacres. There was much effervescence in the town. Groups were talking excitedly. Herbert and I were crazy for news. The last we heard was that Mahmud Shevket Pasha's army was moving on Constantinople. The regiments lined the main street on the way to the railway station. Something was going on—we could not tell what. Suddenly they cheered—all together. The cheering was taken up by the crowd. The band began to play. The regiments wheeled from attention, and continued their march.

We went into a Greek shop. "What does all this mean?" we asked. The proprietor eyed us in astonishment. "Don't you understand?" he answered. "Abdul Hamid has been deposed, and his imprisoned brother proclaimed *sultan*. The soldiers are cheering for Mohammed V. The authorities here kept back the news. They didn't want to make the announcement until the troops unquestionably loyal to the New *Régime* were landed."

There was much anxiety during the rest of the afternoon. The Christians were nervous, Greeks and Syrians as well as Armenians. The British have landed a few marines, and established a wig-wag station on top of a house near us. People began to come for refuge to the American mission at nightfall.

We have rumours of a second massacre at Adana this morning.

Chapter 12

The Young Turks and the Toy Fleet

Mersina,
April twenty-ninth.

Dear Mother:

I suppose that baby doesn't come because I'm too busy and the time is not propitious. There are more important things to think about and to do. Sounds unmaternal and abnormal, doesn't it? But just like other girls I had my dreams of how these days of waiting would be. And up to several weeks ago I plied the needle vigorously, and thought a lot about how many of each wee garment would be necessary, and what sort of blanket would wash best. I hesitated a long time before deciding which dress was the prettiest for *it* to be baptized in. Now I don't know how many garments I have. I haven't even made a complete inventory of what we brought from Tarsus. We are too engrossed in the duties and problems that each day brings forth to think at all about the morrow. Honestly, Mother, during the four days we have been in Mersina, maternity hasn't had much of a place in my mind—I mean, of course, my own maternity. Heaven knows we have the babies coming in abundance all the time around us, and there is everything to be done for them.

I wrote you of the landing of the Turkish regiments from Beirut on the day we learned of Abdul Hamid's deposition. They went to Adana the same day, and started that night a second massacre more terrible than the first. The Armenians had given up their arms. On the advice of the foreign naval officers—trusting in the warships here at Mersina—they accepted the assurance of the government that the "rioting" was over. So they were defenceless when the Young Turk regiments came. The butchery was easier. I spare you details. I wish to God I could have spared them to myself. Most of our Adana friends who escaped the first massacre must have been killed since last Saturday. The few who have reached Mersina are like the messengers that came to Job. Adana is still hell. The soldiers set fire to the French Mission buildings, and are going each night after other foreign property. The American Girls' Boarding School was evacuated. The teachers and some girls who were saved arrived yesterday, and are with us. One of our American teachers has typhoid, and reached us on a stretcher.

Herbert brought me here from Tarsus to get away from the contagion that might come from the crowding of refugees in our compound. It is now worse here than it was in Tarsus. And this morning word came to us that we must be ready at any moment to move to the French Consulate. The captains of the war-ships had a meeting last night, and decided to defend the French and German consulates in case of trouble. They notified the local authorities that if killing began in Mersina three hundred German, French and British sailors would be landed with machine-guns *to protect foreigners*. The idea is to gather the foreigners together, and let the Armenians and other native Christians shift for themselves. Of course we could not enter into any such scheme as that.

The Dodds would under no circumstances desert those who have taken refuge with them. Anyway, we Americans are invited only by courtesy. Ships of the other Great Powers are here. American ships are supposed to be *en route*. But we have not seen them yet. We wonder if the new administration is going to continue the supine policy of Mr. Roosevelt, who always refused to do anything for Americans and American interests in this part of the world. I used to think that missionaries looked to Washington for help and protection. Now I know that the United States is known in Turkey only by the missionaries. If our flag has any prestige or honour, it is due to men like Daddy Christie, and not to the embassy in Constantinople or the few consuls scattered here and there.

At the station, soldiers are turning back the Armenians who have managed to slip into trains at Adana and Tarsus. From a long distance one can see, when riding in the train, the warships in the harbour, flying the flags of the "protecting" powers, whose obligation to make secure life and liberty for Armenians was solemnly entered into by the Treaty of Berlin. One does not expect much of Russia: the treaty was imposed upon her. But England, France, Germany, Austria, Italy— they all have war-ships at Mersina. Armenian refugees, fleeing from the massacre at Adana, which occurred right under the nose of the

English, French, Germans, Austrians and Italians, see these warships as the train draws into Mersina station. Turkish soldiers, of the same regiments who massacred them three days ago, bar the way. Back they must go to death.

Herbert and I meet the trains. We look for the chance to smuggle friends through. We got H—— B—— through yesterday. The Swiss stationmaster, Monsieur B——, remonstrated hotly with Herbert about allowing me to come to the station. "It is no place for your wife," he declared. "There might be bloodshed any minute, if a refugee resists."

But I held my ground. I knew H—— B—— was going to try to get on this train. He had money to bribe with, and could travel first-class. Mother, I managed to slip into the first-class coach just as the train stopped, and came out the other end leaning heavily on H—— B——'s arm. We left the station through the waiting-room, and none said a word or stopped us. H—— B—— was safe. Herbert couldn't have done it. The Turks, for all their cruelty, have a curious chivalry upon which I banked. I was not mistaken. H—— B—— kept my arm all the way to the Dodds. The poor boy is in agony. He has just heard that his father, a wealthy merchant of Alexandretta, was killed, and his mother and sister—well, I'll leave it to you to guess.

But this adventure is nothing to one I had late in the afternoon of the twenty-seventh. Herbert had gone for news to the wigwagging station the British have established on a villa just in front of Major Doughty-Wylie's. I thought there might still be some oranges in the bazaar. It was an excuse to walk. I cannot stay indoors—no matter what happens. It wasn't far, anyhow. Just a little way down our street. As I was returning, I heard "Won't you come home, Bill Bailey," coming from somewhere. It struck me as curious. I stopped. The whistling continued *staccato* and insistent. It came from a narrow side street. I waited until the patrol had passed along, and then whistled in turn, "Every night the papers say," and stopped. Immediately it was taken up: "There's a robbery in the park." I decided to investigate.

Several houses along, I heard a whisper, "Mrs. Gibbons." Under the stoop was an American Armenian, whom I had met during the winter in Adana. He had been waiting for someone he knew to pass on the main street. He was in rags—had worked his way overland somehow from Adana. He would be arrested if he tried to make the Mission. Patrols were passing constantly. I told him to wait where he was. I went back to the Dodds, put on Herbert's raincoat, stuffed a cap in the pocket, and returned to the side street. The Armenian refugee could cover himself completely in the coat. I told him to pull the cap well down over his ears. He walked back with me. It was no trouble at all. The young man has money, and an American passport. The latter is no good to him. As he can pay, we think it possible to smuggle him somehow aboard a ship.[1]

Almost all who have reached Mersina, however, are women and children. For the men are killed on sight. The refugees in the Dodds' compound are of my sex. They are husbandless, fatherless, sonless. Now we know that the only difference between Young and Old Turks is that the Young Turks are more energetic and thorough in their massacring. None would succeed in escaping the dragnet were it not for the fact that Armenians look and dress—and many of them speak—just like Turks. Refugees are not easily detected.

My doctor has gone. The day after we reached Mersina, he had a chance to get passage with his family to Cyprus. I urged him to go. I had Miss Talbot, and I could not have on my mind the responsibility of his remaining just to take care of me. I am glad he left when the going was good. Now it is practically impossible. The *scal,* from which the little boats go out to the ships, is carefully guarded. The Young Turks are taking "strict measures" to put down "the rebellion!" Armenians who try to escape from the Adana butcher's pen are hauled before the court-martial. According to the Turkish reasoning, attempting to avoid death is proof of an Armenian's guilt.

As I write these awful things—a few weeks ago I should have called them incredible things—I see from my window the half-moon of war-ships a mile out to sea. They ride quietly at anchor. Launches are all the time plying to and fro between ships and shore. That is the extent of their activity.

---

1. This was afterwards done, but I was unfortunately unable to have a part in it. I think I know one Armenian who believes the U. S. A. is the place to stay forever!

CHAPTER 13

A New Life

Mersina,
May twelfth.

Grandmother dear:

I think it was old Thales (I'm nearer the Greek philosophers out here than I ever was at college) who held that the earth was nothing but certain elements in a state of constant change. Everything is changing all the time. And the inhabitants of the earth have the same chance and luck as the earth, and follow the same law. It is well expressed from the standpoint of the moment of time in which one is placed by the favourite Turkish proverb: "*This also shall pass!*" Typically Turkish, that proverb: for the Turk never interprets any event, never tackles the solution of any problem, except in terms of himself and the present. Yesterday is like tomorrow. It is a waste of time to worry over either. In crises Turkish philosophy is excellent. It helps a lot to create nerve and maintain fortitude if only you can keep saying to yourself with conviction: "This also shall pass!"

Scrappie is beside me as I write, in the reed basket we bought from the *fellahin*. I am propped just high enough on the pillows to keep my eye on her. I watch her all the time to see if she is really breathing. I have heard of wives making husbands get up in the night to see if baby was breathing, and scoffed at the folly of it. But I'm going to confess to you that I've had two panics. Each time I assured Herbert that this happens only with first babies, but that doesn't seem to mollify him. There never was such a fellow for sleeping as Herbert. However, wouldn't it be awful if the baby's covers got up over her head? You understand how I feel, don't you?

Miette, "bread-crumb," is the name Jeanne Imer gave Christine in prospect. It also means a little scrap of anything: so Herbert and I translated it into Scrappie. The name had the advantage of being non-committal on sex. So Scrappie she is to us. Perhaps you will give her another pet name in Paris. But we rather like ours—I never heard of another kiddie having it.

The birth of your grandchild was not a whit less dramatic than the events preceding. There was a "situation" right up to the last. I wrote you about the plan to gather foreigners in two defended consulates if there was a new massacre at Mersina. The massacre didn't come off. We shouldn't have gone anyway. Miss Talbot was as game as we were to stay on with the Dodds. The improvised hospitals in Adana called for all available medical men. The ship surgeons, with their pharmacists, all went to Adana. The Mersina mission doctor was working among our Tarsus wounded. I was altogether doctorless. At daybreak of Scrappie's birthday, Mr. Dodds swept the horizon of the sea with his telescope. We were expecting every day relief ships, with Red Cross units, from Beirut. A speck developed into a steamer. Without waiting to ascertain more, Mr. Dodds threw himself into his row-boat. Two husky servants of the mission were at the oars.

It was lucky Mr. Dodds did not hesitate longer. But he is not that sort. It was a ship from Beirut, and there was an American surgeon aboard. Doctor Dorman walked into my room just in time.

Everybody in the Mission feels that the placid little baby, with her great blue eyes, is the symbol of hope. Scrappie knows nothing of what the wicked world is doing and how all around her are dying and suffering. She is unadulterated joy. Miss Talbot tried her best, but there were no drawn blinds and pale wan mother. Folks came in to offer congratulations, and make a fuss. I was glad they did. The refugees in the compound celebrated by gathering on a roof below and singing. Some were sorry for us, because it was not a boy, but, after all, if *Madama* wanted a girl—how queer of Americans to be glad to have daughters!

No one around the Mission had time to celebrate with Herbert, and there was nothing anyway to drink the baby's health in. Herbert went out to send telegrams to the Doughty-Wylies and the Christies, and the cablegram to the Estes. He says he kept saying to himself as he went down the street, "I'm a father!" It's like men to be proud and take all the credit, which just now I think belongs to me. Herbert went to the British wigwag station, but the sailors couldn't leave their post. So he had to order a bottle of beer at Flutey's all alone. Just then a German lieutenant drifted in. Herbert told him the good news, although he had never seen him before, and he drank the toast as sympathetically as a young bachelor could. [1]

On the morning of Scrappie's advent, after a hurried breakfast, my doctor rushed for the Adana train. I haven't seen him since. Nor any other doctor. Miss Talbot is superb. I couldn't have better care. Mrs. Dodds cooks for me herself, and serves my meals. She thinks Miss Talbot is over-careful in prescribing my diet. When Mrs. Dodds brings soft-boiled eggs, she whispers: "Eat half of this quickly. Miss Talbot thinks there is only one, but I'd like to see any one go hungry in Belle Dodds' house!" Until today, when I am first able to write you, they kept pillows out of my reach—books, too.

Herbert is too busy to be with me. He has had to go to Tarsus and twice to Adana. Two days after Scrappie came, the major telegraphed for him to come to take the witness-stand before the court-martial. Lawson Chambers had gone on relief work in the interior, and Herbert was the only other foreigner who saw the beginning of the massacre. It was a risky business, but I have got used to letting him go. The tragedy is too great for individuals to count—or to think of themselves.

With Herbert away, and Scrappie sleeping most of the time, and no books, all I could do was to sing. I've gone over all my favourite songs—and many that weren't favourites have been hummed through to the end. I refused to be deterred by the fact that I am under a roof where singing is mostly confined to the metrical version of the Psalms. Mr. Dodds, however, gets away bravely from psalms when he comes to sit beside me of an evening. He loves to hold Scrappie, and sing to her, "Shut Down the Curtains of Your Sweet Blue Eyes." Herbert delights her with "Macnamara's Band."

I have had other visitors in this first week. Most welcome was the chaplain of the British cruiser *Swiftsure*, of whom we had seen something before Scrappie arrived. (Note how I date everything by Scrappie?) Scrappie was about fifty hours old when he turned up with a bottle of old brandy under his arm. I was glad to have his call—and the bottle—just as Herbert was going off once more. And with my door open—it could not be shut all the time—I could hear those dreadful telegrams being read that kept coming from Kessab, Dortyol," Hadjin and other towns of our *vilayet* and of Northern Syria. Everywhere it was the same story.

---

1. A year later I told this story in a Berlin *salon*. One of the guests at tea, Countess ——, exclaimed, "Why that boy was my son. He wrote me about it at the time."

Yesterday a second American battle cruiser arrived. It was the *Montana*. The *North Carolina* came in several days ago. The first officer to land from the *Montana* was Lieutenant-Commander Beach. When he came to the Mission to call, I asked Miss Talbot to bring him in. He stayed some time, and would have cheered me up a lot had he not mentioned that Lili Neumann was dead. He did not know, of course, what Lili was to me, and I managed to say nothing. Under other circumstances it would have been a bad shock, but just now nothing seems to go too deep. However, my face must have told him I was suffering, for he looked down so kindly, and asked if there was anything I wanted. "Because, by Jove! you can have the ship," he declared. I told him I hadn't seen ice for ten months. "Just the thing," he exclaimed. A few hours later, sailors brought a huge rectangle of the most delicious thing in the world. There was also a bottle of *Bols curaçao*, and a sweet note. People are good.

Mr. Dodds and Mr. Wilson and Herbert got to work on the ice with hatchets. Mrs. Dodds made ice-cream last night and again for lunch today.

I must stop this letter, which has been written largely on the inspiration of that ice-cream. Miss Talbot has scolded me twice, and she hasn't seen other times that I got the paper and pencil under the mattress too soon for her. I cannot leave it, though, without telling you of another invaluable helper. The very day of Scrappie's arrival, a wee, sawed-off Armenian woman came in. I heard somebody say "Sh," but she started in her toothless Jabberwocky. Miss Talbot tried the effect of cool, insistent English, but she couldn't put Dudu Hanum out. For Dudu Hanum squatted down on the floor, and I snickered. Miss T. thought I was asleep. She went to get Mrs. Dodds to interpret. In the meantime, Dudu Hanum addressed me. She rolled up her sleeves and held her arms out and then up over her head the way you do when you want to stop hiccoughs. All the while she talked volubly. It wasn't Turkish.

I had learned some of that. As it didn't sound like a gang of wreckers pulling down a house, it wasn't Arabic. Must be Armenian. I recognized Dudu Hanum as the sister of the agent who gets our things out of the custom-house. Finally we learned what it was all about. Dudu Hanum was saying: "I have no gift to give you, but I have these two hands. Let me do your washing. I shall wash all your things and all of the baby's." The blessed old thing comes early every morning. What garments Mrs. Dodds allows to escape from her own capable hands, Dudu Hanum washes, and hangs them to dry upon the sun-baked roof.

CHAPTER 14

Off to Egypt

May twenty-seventh.

Granny Dear:

"The force of example" was a dry old phrase to me not longer than twenty-one days ago. But since Scrapple's coming has moved the generations in our family back one whole cog, I have been thinking about that phrase as something vital. If I continue to call you "Mother," Scrappie will call you that. Must I also begin now to call Herbert "father"—move him back a generation, too?

I feel as if I had *always* had Scrappie. We are not yet at the end of May. But April seems ages ago. The mail from America is just coming with stories of the massacres, and what I read seems unreal. Most of it is. The stories about us are absurd. We never "fled to the coast." We sent but one cablegram to Philadelphia, and none at all to Hartford. That cablegram contained only the single word "safe" to relieve your anxiety. I see now what that anxiety must have been. So you read that Tarsus was wiped off the map? It would have been—had not the wind changed that night.

Since I have been quietly resting, stretched out on my back, I have decided to put April, 1909, out of my life. Herbert and I do not want to share each other's memories. We have not told each other all we have seen—nor even all we felt and all we did. I cannot get Herbert's full story from him. He does not ask for mine.

Of course, we cannot escape the result of the events we have lived. Just as Herbert's hair has become so white, there must be something inside of us changed, too. Time alone will tell that. Only one thing we do realize right now,—our responsibility to the Armenians. We must work in Egypt, in France, in Germany, in England—and, perhaps later, in America—to let the world know how the Armenians have suffered and what their lot must always be under Turkish rule. We see too—oh, so clearly—how heartless and cynical the diplomats of Europe are. They are the cause, as much as the Turks, of the massacres. Not the foreign policy of Russia or Germany alone. As far as the Near East goes, the Great Powers are equally guilty. No distinction can be drawn between them. In England, in Germany and in France, people do not care—because these horrible things are done so far away. They are indifferent to their own solemn treaty obligations. They are ignorant of the cruelty and wickedness of the selfish policy pursued by the men to whom they entrust their foreign affairs. I see blood when I think of what is called "European diplomacy"—for blood is there, blood shed before your eyes.

We are looking forward eagerly to having you join us in France next month. We shall not talk of the massacres, to you or to any one, except so much as is necessary to help the Armenian Relief Fund and to show the wickedness and faithlessness of the diplomacy of the Powers in Turkey. Herbert and I have been saved, and we have our blessed baby. Our life is ahead of us—we are glad to have it ahead—and we want to spend our time and energy in meeting new duties, in solving new problems. Perhaps that is the spirit of youth. But then we are young, and what interests us is our baby's generation. The new life dates from May 5th, when she came to us.

Dear, dear, you would never guess from this long letter I am writing what is going to happen this afternoon. I am able to write only because of the stern orders I got from the boss this morning. He has immobilized me. I am lazily resting in bed just as if I hadn't been up yet at all. My bed is an island, entirely surrounded by luggage. Suitcases are nearest me. Trunks and steamer bundle are by the door. A Russian steamer is due to leave this evening. Herbert has taken passage on her as far as Beirut. There we shall catch the Italian leaving Saturday, or perhaps the Messageries *Portugal*, scheduled for Monday.

Fancy going to Egypt to get cool in summer! Most people go there to get warm in winter. Our year is finished. We meant to go early in June, anyway. It is a good thing I am feeling so well, and got my strength back so quickly. The heat is coming on, and we fear quarantine at Beirut and Port Said, if an epidemic breaks out here. This is an urgent reason for our going immediately. Herbert turned over night from a college professor to a newspaper man. He has managed to send dispatches by little boats to Cyprus and they have gone uncensored to Paris. But now he has done all that needs to be done here in the way

87

of getting news out. Much good has been accomplished by publicity.

If you didn't have me here to think about when you opened your newspaper at the breakfast table, you would just read headlines, and say, "the Armenians are in trouble again." By "you" I mean the average person at home. Now what Herbert and I must do is to tell our story and give our testimony as convincingly as we can, and then put it where the most people can see it. We detest the advertisement from a personal standpoint, but cannot consider that now.

S. S. *Assouan*
Off the Cilician Coast,
Friday night.
May twenty-seventh.

It wasn't a Russian steamer after all, but an old tub of a *Khedivial*. It is a palace to us, however, and the British flag looks good to Americans.

The last thing that happened to us in Turkey was to have Scrappie christened. Dr. Christie and Mother Christie came down to say goodbye, and Socrates with them. The new American Consul had just arrived from Patras. (He turned out to be a college classmate of Herbert's!) A christening party was improvised for our farewell. So Scrappie got her name, Christine Este, and the consul gave a combination birth and baptismal certificate, with the eagle stamped upon it. I wore my blue dimity dress. Herbert put a big rocking-chair behind me, so that I could flop down in it the first minute I felt tired. Scrappie wore the prettiest of her long dresses, and under her chin was tucked an Indian embroidered handkerchief that Mrs. Doughty-Wylie had long ago given me against the christening day.

It was an odd gathering, missionaries, English and American naval officers, sailors from the warships, Armenian friends, some of our boys, including Socrates, and others I did not know who came to help eat the cake and drink the sherbet. In the Orient, one's door is open to all the world at a feast. I got nervous only when they wanted to kiss the baby. Scrappie howled, and I was glad of the excuse to withdraw her.

When I went downstairs to the carriage, one of the officers of the *North Carolina* carried my bag, and drove me to the *scala*. Mother Christie held Scrappie. The *North Carolina's* launch was waiting. Out we went to the great ship, where I was to spend the afternoon. The Christies and others were coming later to say goodbye. Herbert was to spend the afternoon rounding up the baggage with the help of

Socrates, and row it out to the *Assouan*. A London war correspondent had just arrived, too—the first of the newspaper men—and Herbert had to pilot him around.

The sky-line of Mersina, broken by the minarets, gleamed white in the sunshine. I did not dare to think too hard about what I was leaving. My mind flew back to the day I left Tarsus, how the Armenian women pressed my hands, touched my dress as I passed, and made me promise to come back. I cheered up by looking at the American flag waving from the stern of the launch. Only a year ago, and that was the *natural* sight. I did not know that Tarsus and Mersina existed. Turkey was something I thought would forever be vague. And now—it has become a part of my life. All right to talk about banishing memories. But could we? The sunshine of the East they say casts its spell forever over those who have lived in it. Would we ever comeback?

We steamed for a mile straight out to sea. The officers told me I was in command, and jollied along as if I were not a matron with a baby. One ensign, a Southerner, of course, called me "Miss" with that inimitable drawl. He was just the kind who would have made it "sweetheart" in an hour. I felt a bit shaky when the launch drew up beside the gleaming white cruiser. As we reached the ladder and then fell away, I imagined my baby falling into the water. First touch of maternal worry, which I suppose I shall now have for the rest of my life. The lieutenant-commander took the baby. Two ensigns carried me up. Once on that ship I was at home.

The captain was waiting to greet the youngest girl who had ever been entertained on the *North Carolina*. Scrappie was fixed up in an officer's bunk, where I knew she would sleep just as placidly as ashore until it was time for her next meal. I was invited into the wardroom. A leather armchair and—I ought to write a cup of tea, but it wasn't—awaited me. The officers, of course, knew lots of my friends. My mind went waltzing back to dancing days in the Armoury and to my birthday dinners at the old Bellevue after Army-Navy games. I was living in the anti-Herbert period, when parsons and missionaries and Turkey and babies did not claim me.

There was a soft knock at the steel door that stood ajar. A big negro put in his head, and announced: "Missus, dat chile am cryin'."

I hurried to my responsibility. Beside the bunk, looking down at the tiny mite, stood a *coon* in white linen. "Missus," he said, "de cap'n tole me to keep mah eye on dis li'l baby, an' not even let a fly walk 'cross dat chile's face. I wants yoh t' know, lady, dem's de bes' awdahs dis coon's had sence he lef home. But I couldn't stop it cryin' jes' now."

As I picked up Scrappie, whose great blue eyes shelter no shadow of the hell that came so near, I realized, with a wave of happiness overwhelming me, that I alone could quiet her.

Late in the afternoon Herbert came with Miss Talbot and the Dodds and Christies. They accompanied us to the *Assouan* in the launch. It was hard to say goodbye to the women who had been nearest during the days of danger and suffering. Mother Christie held Scrappie to the last moment. Miss Talbot, my faithful nurse, who had stuck by me for seven weeks with unwavering devotion when there was so much larger and so much more tempting a field in nursing the wounded—what could I say to her? Jeanne Imer and Mary Rogers had been with me constantly. I expected to see them soon again in Europe. But Mrs. Dodds, who had taken me in and done for me as if I were one of her own family—was I just to say "Thank you!"? I said to Mrs. Dodds: "What can I ever do for you to—to—"

She gently interrupted. "You don't know life, dear, if you think you can do anything for me. You will probably never see me again. If you ever meet a woman having a baby under difficult circumstances—just help her!"

LEONAUR

ALSO FROM LEONAUR
AVAILABLE IN SOFTCOVER OR HARDCOVER WITH DUST JACKET

THE WOMAN IN BATTLE by Loreta Janeta Velazquez—Soldier, Spy and Secret Service Agent for the Confederacy During the American Civil War.

BOOTS AND SADDLES by Elizabeth B. Custer—The experiences of General Custer's Wife on the Western Plains.

FANNIE BEERS' CIVIL WAR by Fannie A. Beers—A Confederate Lady's Experiences of Nursing During the Campaigns & Battles of the American Civil War.

LADY SALE'S AFGHANISTAN by Florentia Sale—An Indomitable Victorian Lady's Account of the Retreat from Kabul During the First Afghan War.

THE TWO WARS OF MRS DUBERLY by Frances Isabella Duberly—An Intrepid Victorian Lady's Experience of the Crimea and Indian Mutiny.

THE REBELLIOUS DUCHESS by Paul F. S. Dermoncourt—The Adventures of the Duchess of Berri and Her Attempt to Overthrow French Monarchy.

LADIES OF WATERLOO by Charlotte A. Eaton, Magdalene de Lancey & Juana Smith—The Experiences of Three Women During the Campaign of 1815: Waterloo Days by Charlotte A. Eaton, A Week at Waterloo by Magdalene de Lancey & Juana's Story by Juana Smith.

NURSE AND SPY IN THE UNION ARMY by Sarah Emma Evelyn Edmonds—During the American Civil War

WIFE NO. 19 by Ann Eliza Young—The Life & Ordeals of a Mormon Woman During the 19th Century

DIARY OF A NURSE IN SOUTH AFRICA by Alice Bron—With the Dutch-Belgian Red Cross During the Boer War

MARIE ANTOINETTE AND THE DOWNFALL OF ROYALTY by Imbert de Saint-Amand—The Queen of France and the French Revolution

THE MEMSAHIB & THE MUTINY by R. M. Coopland—An English lady's ordeals in Gwalior and Agra during the Indian Mutiny 1857

MY CAPTIVITY AMONG THE SIOUX INDIANS by Fanny Kelly—The ordeal of a pioneer woman crossing the Western Plains in 1864

WITH MAXIMILIAN IN MEXICO by Sara Yorke Stevenson—A Lady's experience of the French Adventure